AF679801

PRAISE FOR *CORE CALM™*

The Core Calm™ Nature-Based Therapy curriculum, developed by Lindsay A. Cray, is a thoughtfully designed and clinically grounded resource for practitioners working with trauma and nervous system regulation. The curriculum skillfully integrates neuroscience, trauma-informed care, and established ecotherapy interventions, applying them in a way that is both accessible and clinically meaningful. Each lesson is rooted in evidence-informed theory and designed for adaptability across diverse client populations. Drawing from Acceptance and Commitment Therapy (ACT), mindfulness, and ecotherapy, Core Calm™ equips clinicians with practical interventions, progress-monitoring tools, and structured resources that support integration into comprehensive treatment planning.

A notable strength of this model is its emphasis on clinician-led psychoeducation paired with experiential skill-building, enhancing clients' ability to transfer insights beyond the therapeutic setting. Organized into 12 cohesive sessions, the curriculum offers a clear, theoretically sound framework that supports healing, growth, and sustainable nervous system regulation.

— **Dr. Christine Lynn Norton, LCSW-S, CCAT, CCTP, CET**

Core Calm™ offers a structured and highly adaptable framework that translates effectively into real-world outdoor programming, particularly within veteran and first responder populations. Its session-based design allows non-clinical outdoor leaders to facilitate meaningful, skills-based experiences that reinforce mindfulness, emotional regulation, and reflective practice—while maintaining appropriate clinical boundaries.

The model excels in bridging the gap between licensed clinicians and field-based staff. By providing a shared language, clear structure, and alignment with CBT and ACT principles, Core Calm™ enables outdoor leaders to function as competent and ethical extenders of care within multidisciplinary teams. This enhances program cohesion without compromising clinical integrity.

From a program development and risk management perspective, Core Calm™ strengthens consistency, supports staff training, and promotes safe, intentional delivery in dynamic outdoor environments. It is a credible, practical, and highly applicable resource for organizations seeking to elevate the quality and impact of nature-based therapeutic programming.

— **Aaron Leonard, Former U.S. Army Officer | Nonprofit Executive | Guardian Revival**

CORE CALM
1:1 NATURE-BASED THERAPY

Integrating Nature

CORE CALM™: 1:1 Nature-Based Therapy
The Clinician's Guide for Transforming Mental Health Through Nature Immersion

© 2026 by **Integrating Nature Mental Health Counseling, PLLC**

All rights reserved.

No part of this publication may be reproduced, distributed, transmitted, stored in a retrieval system, or used in any form or by any means—electronic, mechanical, photocopying, recording, or otherwise—without the prior written permission of the publisher, except in the case of brief quotations used in reviews, scholarly work, or educational citation with proper attribution.

This manual is intended for educational and professional training purposes only. It is not a substitute for clinical judgment, professional training, licensure, or supervision. The author and publisher assume no responsibility for any outcomes resulting from the use or misuse of the material contained within this guide.
The Core Calm™ model and associated materials are proprietary intellectual property of Integrating Nature Mental Health Counseling, PLLC. Unauthorized use, reproduction, or distribution of Core Calm™ materials, frameworks, or program structures is strictly prohibited.

Nature-Based Therapy (NBT), ecotherapy practices, and outdoor clinical interventions described in this guide should be implemented only by appropriately trained and qualified professionals. Users are responsible for adhering to all applicable ethical, legal, and safety standards within their scope of practice.

Author:
Lindsay A. Cray, LMHC-D, NCC, CCAT

Publisher:
Integrating Nature Mental Health Counseling, PLLC

First Edition, 2026

Disclaimers
The information provided in this workbook is based on current research and clinical practice at the time of publication. While every effort has been made to ensure accuracy, the author and publisher make no warranties regarding completeness or applicability for specific situations.
Outdoor and nature-based activities carry inherent risks. Practitioners are responsible for conducting proper risk assessments, obtaining informed consent, and ensuring appropriate safety measures are in place.

Trademarks
Core Calm™ is a trademark of Integrating Nature Mental Health Counseling, PLLC. All other trademarks referenced in this publication are the property of their respective owners.

ISBN

979-8-9959942-0-6

In Memory of

Thomas J. Cray

Veteran, Leader, Servant, and Father

PREFACE

Mental health treatment has historically emphasized cognitive, behavioral, and intrapersonal processes within controlled, indoor environments. While these approaches are effective, they often overlook a critical dimension of human functioning: our inherent relationship with the natural world.

The Core Calm™ model was developed to address this gap.

At its foundation, Core Calm™ recognizes that well-being is not solely an internal process, but a relational one—shaped by interactions between individuals, their environments, and broader ecological systems. This perspective is supported by research in ecotherapy, environmental psychology, and mind–body medicine, which consistently demonstrate the regulatory and restorative effects of nature on physiological and psychological functioning.

This guide presents a structured, 12-session Nature-Based Therapy (NBT) framework for licensed clinicians, integrating evidence-based modalities such as Cognitive Behavioral Therapy (CBT) and Acceptance and Commitment Therapy (ACT) with experiential, outdoor interventions that emphasize sensory engagement, embodied awareness, and meaning-making through direct interaction with natural environments. Organized around three core applications—outdoor skills, sensory experience, and positive introspection—the Core Calm™ approach supports emotional regulation, distress tolerance, cognitive flexibility, and resilience, extending therapeutic work beyond traditional settings. Central to this model is the view of nature not simply as a backdrop, but as an active therapeutic partner—offering nonjudgmental feedback, supporting attention restoration, and promoting nervous system regulation to deepen insight alongside cognitive interventions.

This work is also informed by longstanding Indigenous and Traditional Ecological Knowledge systems, which emphasize relationality, balance, and reciprocity with the natural world. Practitioners are encouraged to approach this model with cultural humility, ethical awareness, and respect for these foundations.

Implementing nature-based clinical work requires thoughtful preparation and adherence to professional standards, including careful attention to safety, accessibility, scope of practice, and ethical responsibility beyond traditional settings. This guide is intended to support—not replace—clinical judgment, training, and supervision, while offering an evidence-informed, experientially grounded framework.

—

Lindsay A. Cray, LMHC-D, NCC, CCAT
Integrating Nature Mental Health Counseling, PLLC

AKNOWLEDGEMENTS

I begin with gratitude to the Earth—for nourishing, sustaining, and giving of itself for humankind. My relationship with this mother comes before all, and it is through this connection that this work exists.

This work was shaped through collaboration with clinicians, colleagues, and partners across mental health, outdoor leadership, and veteran-serving communities. Your feedback, insight, and commitment to integrating nature-based approaches into practice helped refine Core Calm™ into a more grounded and applicable model.

I am deeply grateful to the clients who engaged in this work. Your willingness to step into new environments, explore your internal experiences, and remain present in the process has informed every aspect of this guide. Your experiences continue to guide its evolution. This model is also influenced by longstanding ecological and relational knowledge, including Indigenous and land-based traditions that center connection, balance, and reciprocity. I acknowledge these foundations with respect. I thank my husband and my mother for supporting me with endless patience, wisdom, and love. It is their faith in me that I succeed.

ABOUT THE AUTHOR

Lindsay Cray, LMHC-D, is a licensed psychotherapist, outdoor guide, and clinical consultant specializing in Nature-Based Therapy for trauma recovery and professional practice. With over two decades of experience at the intersection of conservation, experiential education, and mental health counseling, she has pioneered a Nature-Based Clinical Therapy model that supports profound healing through intentional engagement with the natural world. Her work has been especially impactful with military veterans and emergency service professionals navigating PTSD, depression, anxiety, and moral injury.

As a certified hiking guide and wilderness survival specialist, Lindsay brings a rare integration of clinical expertise, outdoor leadership, and land-based practice to both counseling and professional training. Her approach is informed by Traditional Ecological Knowledge and Indigenous healing frameworks learned through long-term collaboration, study, and direct experience with Indigenous teachers and communities in North America and the Amazon basin.

Lindsay provides consultation, education, and program development for clinicians and organizations seeking to incorporate evidence-informed, trauma-responsive, and culturally respectful outdoor interventions into therapeutic practice. Her teaching emphasizes nervous system regulation, embodied healing, relational engagement with place, and ethical implementation in real-world clinical and community settings.

An internationally recognized speaker and educator, Lindsay has presented on Nature-Based Therapy, trauma rehabilitation, and environmental approaches to healing at conferences including the Association for Experiential Education International Conference, the New York State Mental Health Counselors Association, the American College of Lifestyle Medicine's Nature as Medicine Doctors Outdoor Summit, and the United Nations COP15 World Summit on Climate Change.

Through Integrating Nature Mental Health Counseling PLLC, Lindsay offers psychotherapy, training, and consultation designed to support deep personal healing, strengthen ethical clinical practice, and advance the future of nature-centered and culturally responsive mental health care.

TABLE OF CONTENTS

12 NATURE-BASED SESSIONS FOR HEALING

INTRODUCTION

You are beginning a 12-session Nature-Based Therapy program designed to support your client's mental health recovery. This work is not about rushing toward change, but about creating safe, steady contact with the natural world as a trusted partner in healing.

Through each session, you will help your client orient to their body, emotions, and environment in ways that foster regulation, resilience, and connection. By attuning to the rhythms and resources of nature, clients will experience thier own intrinsic learning and can gradually reclaim a sense of safety, strength, and meaning in their lives.

©2026 Integrating Nature Mental Health Counseling, PLLC. All Rights Reserved

12 NATURE-BASED SESSIONS FOR HEALING

WHAT IS CORE CALM™

Research demonstrates the effectiveness of the Core Calm™ approach, yet it is through intentional practice that its deepest value emerges. This training equips outdoor leaders and mental health professionals with practical tools for delivering Nature-Based Therapy (NBT)—a clinical intervention that integrates evidence-based methods with the restorative wisdom of the natural world.

Core Calm™offers more than a framework; it is a powerful approach for enhancing treatment outcomes and supporting personal growth. By drawing on mind–body research and grounding it in the healing capacities of nature, Core Calm™provides a validated pathway for fostering resilience, balance, and lasting change.

INTENT AND PURPOSE OF THIS 12-SESSION GUIDE

This guide will help you navigate your approach to a 12-session program that closely links your clients' progress with nature's symbolism. Nature is the most valuable teacher.

Nature-Based Therapy (NBT) is the primary intervention utilized in this program and is a widely accepted clinical model for assisting with stress-related mental illness, such as anxiety, depression, suicidality, and trauma. Core Calm emphasizes awareness and nonjudgmental presence as intrinsic elements mirroring the natural world. Its unique design was supported by a team of health specialists, crisis responders, traditional healers, and wilderness experts. Treatment is proven to have greater success in sustaining a more positive state of mental health and personal empowerment.

PROVEN IMPACT OF CORE CALM AND ECOTHERAPY

Your clients could see results like others have:

79%

- People saw a decrease in severity of symptoms negatively affecting mindfulness. [1]

69%

- People saw a decrease in severity of PTSD and trauma symptoms. [1]
- Regulated emotions as mind and body become connected.
- Heightened social-emotional awareness and mirroring in nature helps build coping skills to manage stress before trauma responses occurs.

Moreover, regular exposure to nature aids:

55%

- Lower adult mental health risk with childhood green space access. [2]

33%

- Less likely to need/use mental health medications if visiting nature 3-4 times/week. [3]

50%

- Reduction in depressive symptoms. [4]

1) Cray, L., Henry, T. & Stefanovic, N. (2022). Trybe Ecotherapy (TE) for the Veteran Population Final Report (T. Henry, Ed.) Review of Trybe Ecotherapy (TE) for the Veteran Population Final Report.

2) Nace, T. (2019, October 31). Just 20 Minutes Of Contact With Nature Lowers Stress Hormone Levels. Forbes. https://www.forbes.com/sites/trevornace/2019/10/31/study-just-20-minutes-of-contact-with-nature-lowers-stress-hormone-levels/?utm_source=chatgpt.com

3) LaMotte, S. (2023, January 16). Enjoying nature may lessen need for some medications, study finds. CNN. https://www.cnn.com/2023/01/16/health/nature-mental-health-study-wellness/index.html

4) Yeon, P.-S., Jeon, J.-Y., Jung, M.-S., Min, G.-M., Kim, G.-Y., Han, K.-M., Shin, M.-J., Jo, S.-H., Kim, J.-G., & Shin, W.-S. (2021). Effect of Forest Therapy on Depression and Anxiety: A Systematic Review and Meta-Analysis. International Journal of Environmental Research and Public Health, 18(23), 12685. https://doi.org/10.3390/ijerph182312685

CORE CALM AS AN INTERVENTION

Core Calm can be applied as an intervention for clients need structured support to regulate emotions, increase awareness, and build resilience in the face of life's challenges. Grounded in the secondary interventions of Acceptance and Commitment Therapy (ACT) and Cognitive Behavioral Therapy (CBT), Core Calm provides a practical framework for cultivating mindfulness—helping clients acknowledge their circumstances, remain present without judgment, and identify their values. This program is especially effective as an experiential application; it helps clients observe thoughts, emotions, and sensations with curiosity rather than avoidance, tolerating discomfort, clarifying values, and setting meaningful goals, making it an effective guide for outdoor-based therapeutic settings.

©2026 Integrating Nature Mental Health Counseling, PLLC. All Rights Reserved

12 NATURE-BASED SESSIONS FOR HEALING

HOW TO USE THE GUIDE

- The sessions are numbered and sequenced very purposefully to progress your client through the skills. Conducting them in the prescribed order enables the most effective, safe and efficient growth and success for you and your clients.
- The sequence of these 12 sessions is critical, as the topics layer on each other and increase in depth of learning utlizing three essential applications **outdoor skills**, **sensory experiences**, and **positive introspection**.
- Preferably, schedule sessions with your clients every week such that the program takes 12 weeks to complete. However, this also depends on your client's rhythm and comfort.
- Use or adapt the suggested activities to best fit your space, client, and time.

Clients can be assessed for progress through the Core Calm program with use of the *Mindfulness and Coping Skills Scale for Ecotherapy*© survey (MCSS-E). This is a 20-item self-report tool designed to track changes in coping skills within a Nature-Based Therapy setting measuring client progress across six key factors: **Emotional Regulation, Distress Tolerance, Equanimity, Responsibility-Taking, Social Skills, Interpersonal Effectiveness**

*For more information and to purchase the MCSS-E assessment please contact Integrating Nature Mental Health Counseling LLC.

THREE ESSENTIAL APPLICATIONS

Positive Introspection

Creating a bridge of parallels between the processes in nature and life's experiences. Stories and symbolism evoke acceptance, organic thought, personal insight and the development of intuition.

Sensory Experience

Relaxing and diverse sensory stimulations of a natural environment are ideal for working with body awareness and mindful presence.

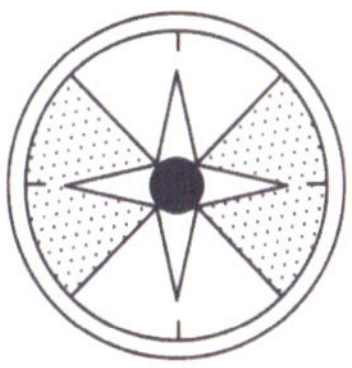

Outdoor Skills

A solution for over stimulation of modern life and screens. Attention is placed firmly in the present to remain in physical engagement with the world while solving for natural consequences.

WHERE TO HOLD SESSIONS

Ideal Locations:

- Park
- Backyard
- Garden
- Roof-top greenspace

Adapting for Inclement Weather:

- Postpone the session until the following meeting and use the current meeting for reflection on previous session(s)
- Have a portion of your office dedicated to live plants and creating an outdoor feel inside

Adapting for Urban Locations:

- Landscaping on the side or back of the building
- Green spaces within a short walk of office
- Travel together or separately to a city park
- Go outside and use vivid pictures, imagery, or transported potted plants

Adapting for Virtual Sessions:

- Use video conferencing on the phone, tablet, or laptop with both the client and you in your own outdoor space

©2026 Integrating Nature Mental Health Counseling, PLLC. All Rights Reserved

12 NATURE-BASED SESSIONS FOR HEALING

COGNITIVE BEHAVIORAL THERAPY (CBT) AS A PASSAGE THROUGH OBSTACLES TO GREATER FUNTIONING

Core Calm integrates CBT principles to build understanding of cognitive functioning, helping you guide clients in recognizing the everyday obstacles that can stand in the way of their goals.

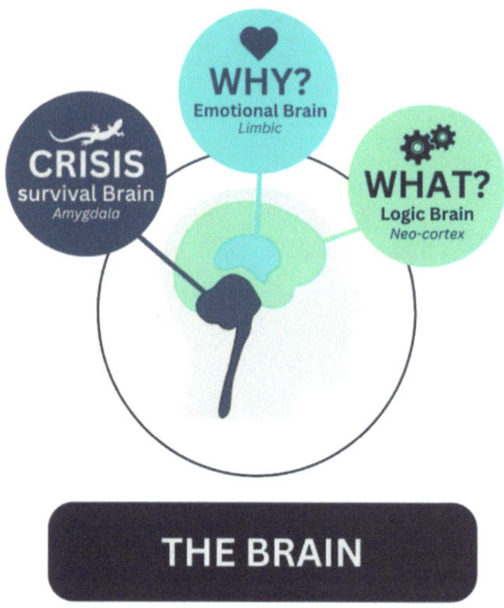

This program begins with helping your clients to normalize barriers to positive functioning. Consider that we are all born with 3 types of brain function;

- **Caring Function**: This function supports our capacity to protect and nurture both ourselves and others. It underlies the motivation to provide care, maintain well-being, and act with compassion.
- **Attachment Function**: This function organizes our need for connection. It enables us to initiate, build, and sustain relationships, reflecting the human drive to seek belonging and to make sense of ourselves through interactions with others.
- **Exploration Function**: This function drives curiosity, courage, and creativity. It motivates us to engage with the world, discover new experiences, and develop personal meaning and purpose.

The amygdala, the brain's *crisis center*, can become conditioned to overreact to stress. When overactive, it overrides the neo-cortex, hijacking logic and the limbic system, hijacking emotional regulation. This disrupts the three core functions: **Caring** may turn into self-neglect or hypervigilance, **Attachment** into distrust or clinging, and **Exploration** into avoidance or impulsivity. Instead of supporting growth and connection, the brain is pulled into survival mode.

You are here to help clients recognize how life's challenges can disrupt their natural functions of **Caring, Attachment,** and **Exploration**. Core Calm begins by normalizing these barriers and reframing them as part of the human experience. When struggles feel overwhelming or "abnormal," clients often turn their frustration inward with self-critical thoughts that diminish confidence and resilience.

Through outdoor activities, reflective practices, and guided discussions, struggles become more manageable because the Neo-cortex and Limbic system of the brain are more frequently accessed. With supportive coping tools, clients strengthen their capacity to care for themselves and others, sustain healthy connections, and step into the world with renewed curiosity and courage. In this way, problems shift from immovable obstacles to opportunities for growth.

©2026 Integrating Nature Mental Health Counseling, PLLC. All Rights Reserved

12 NATURE-BASED SESSIONS FOR HEALING

PREPARING FOR A SESSION

1. Take 30-60 minutes before a session to read and review the curriculum for that day.
2. Select the session location based on weather, space, natural materials, and accessibility. Then visit the site a day or two in advance to ensure it is safe and appropriate.
3. Determine if the content for the session (activities, thoughts, explanations, questions) needs any adjustment.
4. Gather any materials needed for the session and/or identify nearby natural areas to resource them .
5. Practice and do the activities yourself, preferably in the determined location.
6. Take notes on lessons learned from the session to use in future sessions with this client and in using Core Calm with other clients.
7. Carefully consider ways to mitigate and overcome possible risks, areas of resistance and obstacles by reviewing the information below

AREAS OF RISK AND RESISTANCE

IMPORTANT: Clinicians are expected to thoughtfully prepare for risks, resistance, and obstacles when conducting nature-based therapy, while also recognizing that not every scenario can be anticipated and flexibility is essential. This curriculum is intended as a guide to inform best judgment and support safe, ethical practice in outdoor settings. All professionals using it are strongly encouraged to pursue trainings, certifications and licensures in outdoor safety and leadership as well as Leave No Trace ethics to maximize safety for both clients and themselves.

HOW TO MITIGATE AND OVERCOME POSSIBLE RISKS, AREAS OF RESISTANCE, AND OBSTACLES

Cold Weather
Pack warm clothing (non-cotton) with layers, winter hat & gloves, wear appropriate footwear, and bring pocket warmers or a warm beverage such as tea.

Hot Weather
Pack equipment to keep cool (such as a sun hat, ice, water, and neck towels).

Inclement Weather
Have a backup meeting space in case of heavy rain, wind, and extreme heat or cold. This should be an indoor space, unless driving conditions prevent participants from getting to the site (requiring cancellation or video conference).

Common Injuries
Always carry a basic first-aid kit to treat sprains, burns, cuts, and bug bites.

©2026 Integrating Nature Mental Health Counseling, PLLC. All Rights Reserved

NOTES & TAKEAWAYS

My Thoughts & Reflections:

©2026 Integrating Nature Mental Health Counseling, PLLC. All Rights Reserved

SESSION 1

MINDFULNESS

WHY IS THIS IMPORTANT?
Mindfulness can enhance emotional regulation, self-awareness, and stress reduction, ultimately fostering acceptance and improving focus, relationships, and overall well-being.

WHAT YOU NEED TO KNOW IN SUPPORT OF THIS SESSION

BENEFITS OF PRACTICING MINDFULNESS

- Challenges cognitive distortions.
- Helps oneself regulate; By focusing awareness on the breath and body, one acknowledges experiences (positive or negative) without judgment.
- Reduces rumination and symptoms of depression/anxiety, decreases somatic and mental distress, increases working memory and positive affect, improves immune function, and enhances insight, intuition, and fear modulation.
- Increases cognitive and behavioral flexibility, focus, productivity, and relationship satisfaction.

Mindfulness has powerful applications in military, first responder, and civilian settings, demonstrating measurable improvement in treatment.

HOW DOES CORE CALM INCORPORATE MINDFULNESS INTO NATURE-BASED THEREAPY?

Through engagement of body and sensory **awareness** with attention to a natural setting allows one to practice curiosity by creating a space of **acceptance** and **nonjudgment** around an experience. We can witness nonjudgment in ecosystems. For example, trees do not judge - they simply are. Mindfulness helps one develop the ability to **create energetic and mental space to identify and examine dissonance between experiences, values, and current actions**. In this process, nature becomes a mirror reflecting the conscious and unconscious. It brings awareness to and embraces the mindset that nature is all-encompassing; It can thrive and falter yet still be full of life and we can **commit** to this same mindset.

WHAT IS MINDFULNESS?

Mindfulness practice interrupts reactivity and perseveration patterns by bringing attention to the present moment.

"Mindfulness practice may be taught in group or individual settings. Often, there is a pre-and post-evaluation (in reflection or written form) to support awareness of changes during a single practice and over weeks.

Mindfulness is awareness of one's internal states and surroundings. Mindfulness can help people avoid destructive or automatic habits and responses by learning to observe their thoughts, emotions, and other present moment experiences without judging or reacting to them."

American Psychological Association

©2026 Integrating Nature Mental Health Counseling, PLLC. All Rights Reserved

INTRODUCING ACCEPTANCE AND COMMITMENT THERAPY (ACT)

ACT promotes mindfulness by supporting clients in staying present without judgment. In a nature-based setting, the environment becomes a grounding tool for noticing thoughts, emotions, and sensations. By observing internal experiences as one might watch clouds or listen to birdsong, clients learn to accept discomfort and create space for healing. This process opens the way to setting meaningful goals and living in closer alignment with their values.

HOW IS ACT APPLIED IN CORE CALM?

Core Calm combines ACT techniques with mindfulness practices in natural settings to interrupt negative thought patterns and foster new perspectives. Across the 12-session curriculum, clients engage with real-life acceptance exercises and explore the symbolic lessons that nature provides. Using diffusion methods and shifting focus between inner and outer experiences, metaphors from the environment are translated into practical insights.Clients are then guided to express these experiences therapeutically, drawing parallels between natural constructs and their own needs, values, and goals. In this way, nature becomes a personal compass, helping clients orient toward meaningful action and growth.

OUTCOMES OF THIS APPLICATION

People who fixate on past and future worries or struggle to notice the positives of the present often remain caught in a cycle of dissatisfaction. Through a blend of ACT techniques and nature-based examples, Core Calm offers new perspectives that transform stressful events into more manageable and less intimidating challenges. Rather than triggering fight-or-flight reactions or avoidance, the program fosters self-awareness, encourages conscious decision-making, and committment to values-driven actions that lead toward meaningful goals..

TREATMENT GOALS

After completing this session, the client will be able to reflect on their lived experiences and actions with greater meaning and coherence. They will experience the shift from hyper-analyzing and overthinking to sensing, approaching, and reassessing.

GOALS OF THE SESSION

Our goals for this session are to learn about and practice mindfulness.

- The client will understand mindfulness as *purposely paying attention without judgment and noticing without reacting.*
- The client will be able to draw on the act of *living in the present moment* using the natural metaphor of birds, squirrels, and insects all living in the "here and now." Their attention is focused on the moment and their immediate tasks.

©2026 Integrating Nature Mental Health Counseling, PLLC. All Rights Reserved

SESSION 1 - ACTIVITIES

CATEGORY	Introductory	Integrative	Embodied

Activity 1:1 Noticing the Body

Purpose: Establishing core concepts, practices, and safety.

Time: 10 minutes

Focus: ***Learning***

This foundational mindfulness practice introduces your client to present-moment awareness through gentle, nonjudgmental attention to bodily sensations. Practiced in nature, it supports grounding and emotional regulation, preparing your clients for deeper somatic and ecological engagement.

Therapist Preparation:

- **Site Selection:** Choose a quiet, comfortable outdoor space with minimal distractions and grounding features like soft ground or a nearby tree.
- **Establish Safety:** Briefly check in with your client's emotional and physical state. Normalize any discomfort and remind them to pause or shift focus if needed.

Client Engagement Steps:

1. **Set Intentions:** Invite your client to settle and turn their attention inward.
2. **Engage the Senses:** Ask the client to identify a single area of the body to focus on (e.g., hands, feet, legs or breath).
3. **Observe Internal Shifts:** Offer this frame: "Let's take a few moments to practice noticing. Bring your awareness to one part of your body—perhaps your hands. Without moving or changing anything, simply observe any sensation, pressure, tightness, or texture. If a thought arises, gently note it as 'thought,' and return to the body."
4. **Identify:** Encourage your client to name internal sensations (e.g., "warmth," "tingling," "tightness") softly or silently.

Clinical Framing & Ongoing Practice

- Promotes interoceptive awareness and grounding.
- Reorients attention from cognitive overactivity to somatic presence.
- Useful for transitioning into deeper work or when emotional overwhelm is present.
- May apply in daily practice of noticing sensations in one body part, like feet on the earth or hands at rest.

My notes or thoughts for implementing this session:

©2026 Integrating Nature Mental Health Counseling, PLLC. All Rights Reserved

SESSION 1 - ACTIVITIES

CATEGORY	Introductory	Integrative	Embodied

Activity 1:2 Nature Mandala Creation

Purpose: Applying and personalizing practices; deepening the connection between inner experience and the natural world.

Time: 40 minutes

Focus: ***Applying***

This creative, nature-based practice helps your client explore balance, impermanence, and integration through the symbolic process of co-creating a mandala. It strengthens the relationship between your client's internal landscape and the more-than-human world.

Therapist Preparation:

- **Site Selection:** Choose a quiet, respectful, unpopulated space where the mandala can remain for revisits.
- **Familiarize Yourself:** *What is a mandala?*
  A mandala is a sacred circle of meaning; the word *mandala* comes from Sanskrit, meaning circle or center. While mandalas often appear as circular designs with repeating patterns, they are so much more than just beautiful geometry. Mandalas are visual stories of balance, intention, and spiritual connection. They can be:
  - Geometric and symmetrical
  - Free-form and organic
  - Drawn in circles or squares
  - Created with ink, paint, sand, thread, natural materials (leaves, flowers, berries, nuts, stems etc.) and many other mediums.

  Across traditions, cultures, and time—they've been used to connect with a deeper internal sense of knowing. To learn more try visiting this website: *https://truenortharts.com/what-is-a-mandala/*

Client Engagement Steps:

1. **Set Intentions:** Let go of goals; invite intuitive, playful creation.
2. **Introduce the Concept:** Present a few images of mandalas as examples for your client as you offer some context; "Mandalas are used in many cultures to reflect the interconnectedness of life. Like ecosystems, they show us how balance emerges from diversity and change."
3. **Gather Materials:** Encourage use of natural objects (e.g., stones, leaves, bark).
4. **Engage the Senses:** Guide your client to slow down, noticing color, texture, temperature, and weight while building.
5. **Create:** Place materials in circular forms as a symbolic representation of internal states, balance, and transformation.
6. **Reflect:**
7. Use prompts such as:
   - "What part of your internal experience is reflected in this creation?"
   - "How did the elements of nature collaborate with you today?"

Clinical Framing & Ongoing Practice:

- Fosters presence, self-expression, creativity, and ecological reciprocity.
- Personalizes mindfulness through symbolism and sensory engagement.
- May use journaling, photography, or dialogue to track emotional shifts.
- Revisit the mandala in future sessions to observe environmental and internal changes.

©2026 Integrating Nature Mental Health Counseling, PLLC. All Rights Reserved

SESSION 1 - ACTIVITIES

CATEGORY	Introductory	Integrative	Embodied

Activity 1:3 Sky-to-Earth Awareness Practice

Purpose: Fully internalizing the work; cultivating sustained, intuitive, and relational presence with self, others, and nature.

Time: 10 minutes

Focus: ***Becoming***

This somatic practice invites your client to deepen full-body awareness and internalize therapeutic presence through breath, movement, and orientation to the natural world. It encourages a relational stance with nature as co-regulator and witness.

Therapist Preparation:

- **Assess Client Readiness:** Check that your client is emotionally regulated and physically comfortable enough for movement and somatic focus.
- **Site Selection:** Choose a natural setting with a clear view of the sky and grounded features like trees or stones to support vertical awareness and spatial orientation.

Client Engagement Steps:

1. **Begin with a Grounded Stance:** Invite your client to stand firmly on the earth, eyes open with feet shoulder with apart, Shoes may be on or they can choose to be barefoot (which is preferrable).
2. **Settle into the Breath:** Ask your client to begin with four deep breaths. A slow inhale and exhale can help ground your client center thier awareness on the contact between thier body and the earth.
3. **Orient to the Sky:** Have you client tilt head slowly up to the sky and observe. Use gentle prompts such as "Notice the sky—it's color or movement of the clouds. Let yourself observe without judgment."
4. **Track Internal Shifts:** Use gentle prompts such as "What's different in your breath, mood, or energy now compared to earlier?" to have client notice the tiny, internal shifts in thier body as they settle into this grounded stance.
5. **Return to the Earth:** Guide attention to a chosen natural focal point (e.g., tree, rock, or fire circle).
6. **Integrate with Movement:** Ask your client to rise and stretch, reaching toward the sky, then reaching downward—mirroring the flow between internal awareness and environmental connection.

Clinical Framing & Ongoing Practice:

- Strengthens embodied presence and sense of place.
- Bridges cognitive, emotional, and somatic states.
- Encourages intuitive self-regulation through nature connection.
- May apply as a daily nature-based practice to foster ongoing integration of therapeutic insights.

My notes or thoughts for implementing this session:

©2026 Integrating Nature Mental Health Counseling, PLLC. All Rights Reserved

NOTES & TAKEAWAYS

My Thoughts & Reflections:

©2026 Integrating Nature Mental Health Counseling, PLLC. All Rights Reserved

SESSION 2

SELF-AWARENESS

WHY IS THIS IMPORTANT?
Clients become more aware of their mind-body connection, normalizing a sense of curiosity about the connections between thoughts, emotions and behaviors and thereby decreasing feelings of shame.

WHAT YOU NEED TO KNOW IN SUPPORT OF THIS SESSION

WHAT ARE THE BENEFITS OF PRACTICING SELF-AWARENESS?

- Produces a demonstrated chain of psychopathological events that starts with a situation and continues to automatic thoughts, images, and reactions.
- Helps in self-identification of *core beliefs, cognitive distortions,* and the emotional, physical, and behavioral experiences that result from a thought. This is referred to as a "thought record" when written, challenging automatic thoughts, and rating emotional intensity.
- Complements mindfulness practice flexibly.
- Adapts to serve specific populations such as military personnel, children, geriatric populations, and those who suffer from eating disorders and substance use.

HOW DOES CORE CALM INCORPORATE SELF-AWARENESS INTO NATURE-BASED THERAPY?

Research and life experience show that it is difficult for us to relate well to others if we are unaware of ourselves. Activities facilitated in nature can inspire imagination and invite creative play to fine-tune body awareness. This experience helps us safely and playfully identify conditioned trauma responses - when our body feels stuck. Activation and stabilization of primary physical senses in a nature-based setting become foundational to self-acceptance.

MASLOW'S HIERARCHY OF NEEDS

MINDFULNESS-BASED COGNITIVE THERAPY (MBCT) MODEL

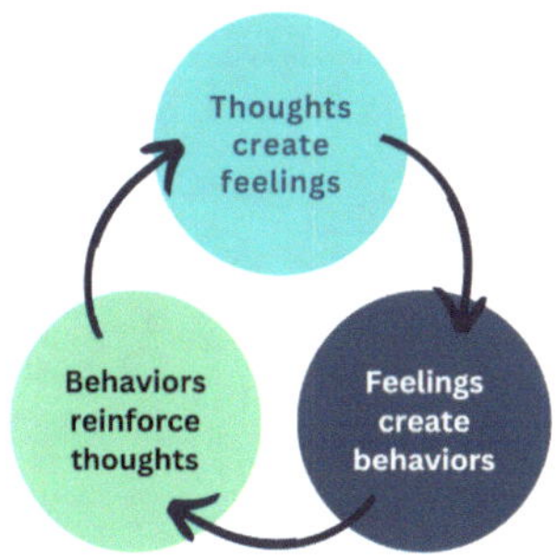

WHAT IS SELF-AWARENESS?

Self-awareness is the ability to understand one's own thoughts, feelings, and behaviors, as well as how they impact oneself and others. It involves recognizing emotions, core beliefs, and reflections on one's strengths and weaknesses to have a more accurate perception of oneself without shame.

Core beliefs are the deep ideas we hold about ourselves, other people, and the world—like "I'm not good enough" or "People can't be trusted." They often run in the background, shaping how we see things without us realizing it. Building self-awareness means noticing these beliefs, asking if they're really true or helpful, and practicing new ways of thinking that support growth and well-being.

©2026 Integrating Nature Mental Health Counseling, PLLC. All Rights Reserved

MINDFULNESS-BASED COGNITIVE THERAPY MODEL (MBCT) AND SELF AWARENESS

Self-awareness is tied to the brain's instinctive drive for survival. Automatic thoughts—shaped by past experiences and core beliefs—are part of the nervous system's threat-scanning process, or hypervigilance. Once vital for detecting danger, this system now often reacts just as strongly to emotional triggers like criticism or exclusion.

These perceived threats can spark anxiety, tension, or a racing heartbeat, even without real danger. Over time, the brain may mislabel everyday stressors as threats, reinforcing patterns of fear or avoidance. The Mindfulness-Based Cognitive Therapy Model helps break this cycle by examining the link between **thoughts**, **feelings** and **behaviors** with **automatic responses** allowing for more intentional, self-aware choices.

TREATMENT GOAL

After completing this session, the client will be able to recognize the Mindfulness-Based Cognitive Therapy Model at work in their minds and bodies as part of building their self-awareness.

GOALS OF THE SESSION

Our goals for this session are to learn about and practice self-awareness using the Mindfulness-Based Cognitive Therapy Model.

- The client will be able to recognize the connection between body and mind working together to make sense of the world. This causes emotional, physical, and behavioral reactions.
- The client will understand the connection between thoughts, emotions, behaviors and physical sensations.

©2026 Integrating Nature Mental Health Counseling, PLLC. All Rights Reserved

SESSION 2 - **ACTIVITIES**

CATEGORY	Introductory	Integrative	Embodied

Activity 2:1 Lemon and the Landscape of Awareness

Purpose: Establishing self-awareness through the cognitive model by linking inner experience with nature-based sensory engagement.

Time: 10 minutes

Focus: ***Learning***

This guided imagery and reflective practice introduces your clients to the foundational components of self-awareness through the Cognitive Model (situation, thoughts, emotions, physical sensations, and behaviors). Using a simple sensory-based lemon visualization, your clients begin to observe how imagined or real-world stimuli activate automatic internal responses. Practiced in nature, this activity builds awareness of cognitive-emotional patterns while grounding the experience in embodied presence.

Therapist Preparation:

- **Learn the Model:** Familiarize yourself with the Mindfulness-Based Cognitive Therapy Model (MBCT) framework, including the five key elements:
  - *Situation*: The external event or experience that triggers a response—this can be something that happens in the moment or something recalled or imagined.
  - *Automatic Thoughts*: The immediate, often unconscious thoughts that arise in response to a situation, shaped by past experiences and internal beliefs.
  - *Emotions*: The feelings that emerge as a result of our situational interpretation, such as fear, sadness, anger, or joy.
  - *Physical Sensations*: The body's physiological response to thoughts and emotions, including changes like tension, increased heart rate, stomach discomfort, or muscle relaxation.
  - *Behaviors*: The actions or reactions that follow—what we do (or avoid doing) as a result of our thoughts, emotions, and bodily sensations.
- **Use a relatable example** (e.g., a flat tire, receiving unexpected news) to illustrate how these elements are linked.
- **Site Selection:** Choose a quiet outdoor location with minimal sensory distractions. A shaded area or spot with a natural focal point (like a tree or patch of earth) can help support embodied grounding.

Client Engagement Steps:

1. **Set Intentions:** Invite your client to settle into the space with a few slow, grounding breaths. Offer this frame: "Today we're exploring how the mind, body, and emotions are deeply connected. By practicing a simple exercise, we'll begin noticing how thoughts can influence what we feel and how our bodies respond."
2. **Guided Visualization:** Use a calm, paced voice and encourage your client to gently close their eyes or lower their gaze:
   "Imagine a basket of fresh lemons resting in front of you.
   Pick one up—notice its weight, its texture.
   Bring it toward your nose and take in the scent—sharp, citrusy.
   Imagine slicing into the lemon—hear the sound, watch the juice release.
   Now bring a slice to your mouth and imagine biting into it. Feel your mouth react."
3. **Pause:** Allow 10–15 seconds for quiet processing.
4. **Observe Internal Shifts:** Use gentle prompts:
   "What did you notice—physically, emotionally, or mentally?"
   "Where in your body did you feel a reaction?"
   "What thoughts, sensations, or memories came up?"
5. **Encourage** your client to name sensations (e.g., "tingling," "warmth," "tension"), emotions (e.g., "surprise," "irritation," joy), and any automatic thoughts or urges.

©2026 Integrating Nature Mental Health Counseling, PLLC. All Rights Reserved

SESSION 2 - **ACTIVITIES**

CATEGORY	Introductory	Integrative	Embodied

Activity 2:1 Lemon and the Landscape of Awareness (Continued)

Clinical Framing & Ongoing Practice

- Helps clients recognize automatic reactions and their root causes.
- Builds the foundation for cognitive restructuring in future sessions.
- Reinforces the mind-body link in nature-based settings.
- Can be returned to in moments of stress to re-map responses.
- This activity introduces the Mindfulness-Based Cognitive Therapy Model experientially by using client observations to map responses to build self-awareness:
  - **Situation**: Imagining the lemon
  - **Automatic Thought**: "This is too sour" or "I remember making lemonade with my grandma"
  - **Emotion**: Surprise, disgust, joy
  - **Behavioral Urge**: Pulling away, swallowing, smiling
  - **Physical Sensation**: Jaw tension, salivation, goosebumps

Use this map to explain how internal experiences are activated in real-life situations, even without external triggers.

Activity 2:2 Meeting the Tree Without Sight

Purpose: Applying and personalizing self-awareness through sensory immersion and memory.

Focus: *Applying*

This experiential activity invites your client to deepen their self-awareness by engaging all senses—except sight—during an intentional encounter with a tree. Temporarily removing visual input amplifies attention to touch, sound, smell, orientation, and intuition. Through this mindful and embodied interaction, your client will begin to notice how perception is shaped by both internal cues and external experience, supporting the development of somatic awareness, memory, and presence.

Therapist Preparation:

- **Site Selection:** Choose a wooded area with space to navigate safely without sight; avoid uneven ground or sharp obstacles.
- **Safety & Consent:** Discuss how your client prefers to be guided and ensure they feel emotionally ready; co-regulate any discomfort related to disorientation.

Client Engagement Steps:

1. **Set Intentions:** Invite your client to close their eyes or wear a soft blindfold and take a few grounding breaths.

- Offer the frame: "Today, we're going to meet a tree in a very different way—through your body's other senses. Without sight, your awareness of texture, scent, sound, and inner response will become your guide. This is an opportunity to practice deep presence and notice how you engage with the world when vision is removed."

2. **Guided Journey:** Gently lead your [sightless] client over a short distance (3–5 minutes walking time) to a tree you've chosen.

- Communicate movements slowly and clearly throughout the walk, ensuring their physical safety. Once at the tree, invite your client to engage with it using all senses except sight. Offer prompts in a calm, exploratory tone:
  - "Place your hands on the bark—is it rough or smooth, wet or dry? Is there moss or sap?"
  - "Explore the tree's shape. Can you feel where it curves, splits, or knots?"

©2026 Integrating Nature Mental Health Counseling, PLLC. All Rights Reserved

SESSION 2 - ACTIVITIES

CATEGORY	Introductory	Integrative	Embodied

Activity 2:2 Meeting the Tree Without Sight (Continued)

- "Stretch your arms outward—can you detect nearby plants or objects?"
- "Try knocking softly on the trunk—what sound does it make?"
- "Notice your feet. What does the ground feel like beneath you?"

Allow 5–7 minutes for your client to explore and internalize this sensory experience.

3. **Return & Reflection:** Gently guide your client back to the starting point, remove the blindfold, and reflect:
   - "What stood out most in your encounter?"
   - "Were there moments of surprise, discomfort, or connection?"
   - "How did your body respond without sight to rely on?"
   - "What inner dialogue or automatic thoughts surfaced?"

After reflection, ask them to attempt to find the tree again on their own, using memory, sensation, and internal cues.

Clinical Framing & Ongoing Practice

- Strengthens interoception and sensory awareness by removing visual input.
- Deepens understanding of how thoughts, emotions, and sensations interact in real time.
- Supports intuitive processing beyond cognitive reasoning through direct nature engagement.
- This activity deepens understanding of the Mindfulness-Based Cognitive Model by removing visual input to allow for amplified experience of the remaining senses.
  - **Situation:** Exploring a tree without sight
  - **Automatic Thoughts:** "I'm unsure," "This feels familiar," "I'm not safe," or "This is exciting"
  - **Emotions:** Curiosity, discomfort, joy, fear
  - **Physical Sensations:** Increased tactile sensitivity, heightened auditory awareness, shifts in balance or breath
  - **Behaviors:** Slowing down, tensing up, or relaxing into the moment

Use this map to integrate sensory awareness with real-life experiences and expand tolerance for the unknown.

My notes or thoughts for implementing this session:

©2026 Integrating Nature Mental Health Counseling, PLLC. All Rights Reserved

SESSION 2 - **ACTIVITIES**

CATEGORY	Introductory	Integrative	Embodied

Activity 2:3 Silent Self-Awareness Walk

Purpose: Internalizing presence through full-body, sensory immersion in nature.

Time: 10 minutes

Focus: ***Becoming***

This solo walk deepens embodied self-awareness by inviting silent, sensory engagement with nature, allowing internal patterns to surface and nature to serve as both mirror and co-regulator.

Therapist Preparation:

- **Site Selection:** Choose a safe, sensory-rich path with a clear route for a 10-minute solo walk.
- **Assess Readiness:** Ensure your client is emotionally and physically prepared; reference prior experiences to support continuity.

Client Engagement Steps:

1. **Set Intentions:** Offer the frame "This walk is an opportunity to meet yourself through your senses. As you move silently through this landscape, let your awareness rest in your body—noticing how you respond to the world around you. What are some *core beliefs* that arise in this quiet moment of introspection?"
2. **Offer Instructions for Silent Walking:**

- "Walk slowly and silently for 10 minutes through the chosen space."
- "Sense the ground beneath your feet, air against your skin, surrounding sounds."
- "Observe thoughts, feelings, and body sensations as they arise."
- "Recognize how core beliefs influence automatic thoughts, emotional reactions, and behaviors- are they accurate or helpful?"
- "Welcome moments of stillness, repetition, or unexpected shifts in energy."
- "If discomfort surfaces, pause and notice it without needing to fix or change it."

Signal the end of the walk gently—by a bell, soft call, or return to a meeting point.

Clinical Framing & Ongoing Practice

- Enhances somatic awareness through movement, breath, and body focus.
- Deepens presence by reducing external distractions and surfacing unconscious responses.
- Embodies the Cognitive Model, linking environment, thoughts, emotions, and body.
- Supports ongoing grounding and emotional regulation through self-inquiry.

My notes or thoughts for implementing this session:

©2026 Integrating Nature Mental Health Counseling, PLLC. All Rights Reserved

Core Beliefs

Objective: Explore the ways in which our core beliefs can be identified and adjusted with self-awareness.

1) Record a core belief that comes to mind during the Silent Self Awareness Walk.
2) Write down the factual information that validates and supports your core belief.
3) Write down the information that cannot be validated and therefore does not support your core belief.
4) Record your adjusted core belief, validated and supported by factual information.

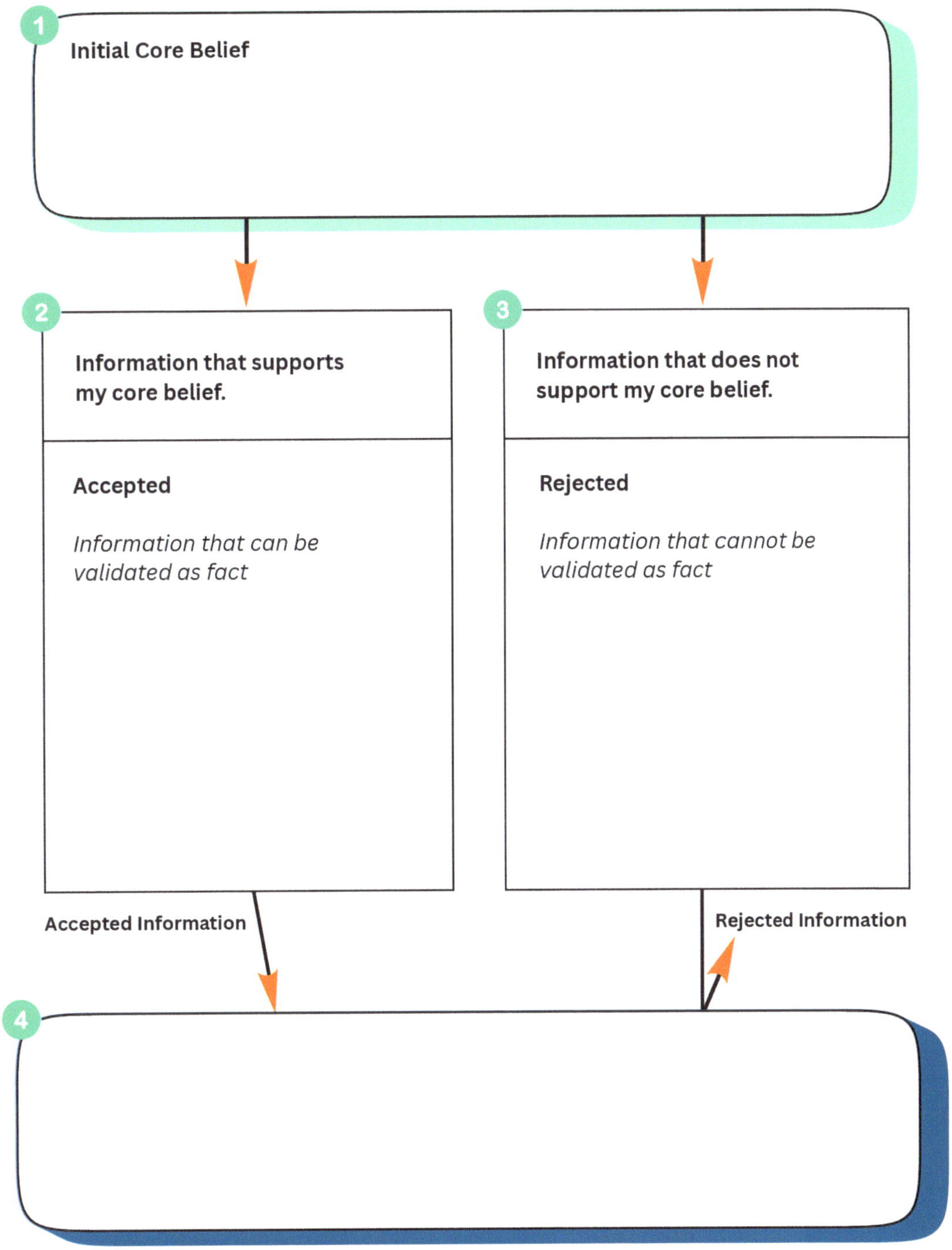

©2026 Integrating Nature Mental Health Counseling, PLLC. All Rights Reserved

NOTES & TAKEAWAYS

My Thoughts & Reflections:

©2026 Integrating Nature Mental Health Counseling, PLLC. All Rights Reserved

SESSION 3

ECOTHERAPY

WHY IS THIS IMPORTANT?
Nature-Based Therapy (NBT), also known as *ecotherapy* can aid clients in developing internal and external resources via nature-based activities to improve emotional functions and life satisfaction.

This session introduces the foundational principles of Nature-Based Therapy (NBT), or *ecotherapy*, as an evidence-based approach that engages nature as an active participant in healing. While earlier sessions may have included outdoor experiences and sensory engagement, this session formally frames those practices within an ecotherapy context. NBT is a broad and evolving field that encompasses therapeutic activities in, with, or through nature—from walking and talking outdoors to stillness, observing natural cycles, or engaging with animals, plants, water, or soil. At its core, ecotherapy fosters a reciprocal relationship between humans and the natural world, where healing and insight are co-created through connection with the more-than-human environment.

Clients are invited to reflect on prior experiences and consider what already aligns with ecotherapy principles. Questions like, "Which activities have felt therapeutic?" or, "How has your body responded after time outdoors versus indoors?" can guide discussion and self-awareness, highlighting the subtle but powerful ways nature supports emotional, physical, and psychological well-being.

WHAT YOU NEED TO KNOW IN SUPPORT OF THIS SESSION

WHAT ARE THE BENEFITS OF PRACTICING ECOTHERAPY?

- Increases relaxation and strengthens self-esteem.
- Decreases depression, blood pressure, and stress.
- Activates the parasympathetic nervous system.

HOW DOES CORE CALM INCORPORATE NATURE-BASED THERAPY INTO PRACTICE?

Core Calm fully embraces relationship with nature in all sessions by contextualizing the outdoor setting as "therapeutic."

WHAT IS ECOTHERAPY?

Ecotherapy is part of ecopsychology and helps clients explore how connecting with the natural world can help to heal them. It uses activities, direction, and opportunities.

Ecotherapy is gaining traction as a means to help people tap into nature's therapeutic powers. The term covers a range of interventions."

"Ecopsychology explores humans' psychological interdependence with the rest of nature and the implications for identity, health, and well-being. Ecopsychology topics include emotional responses to nature; the impacts of environmental issues such as natural disasters and global climate change; and the transpersonal dimensions of environmental identity and concern."

American Psychological Association

©2026 Integrating Nature Mental Health Counseling, PLLC. All Rights Reserved

TREATMENT GOAL

After completing this session, the client will be able to interact with nature as a partner in mirroring real-life obstacles and resourcing necessities, like shelter and fire to symbolize nature's ability to help in the healing process and provide relatable analogies.

GOALS OF THE SESSION

Our goals for this session are to learn about and practice ecotherapy. Your client has already experienced it for the past two sessions via outdoor meetings and immersion, but we have not yet named it.

- The client will understand that *Ecotherapy* is a broad term for *building a mutually beneficial relationship with nature* that may include learning from natural processes and beings such as animals, plants, insects, and so on.
- The client will identify the significant benefits of a relationship with nature for stress, mood, and anxiety management.
- The client can self-select ecotherapy activities such as working with plants, interacting with water, identifying synergistic relationships for food, medicine and utility and observing natural cycles.
- The client understands that they are not independent from nature, rather they have a deeply embedded connection to it (such as calming birdsong and serotonin-inducing barefoot earthing) that aids in connectedness, healing, and self-regulation.

©2026 Integrating Nature Mental Health Counseling, PLLC. All Rights Reserved

SESSION 3 - ACTIVITIES

CATEGORY	Introductory	Integrative	Embodied

Activity 3:1 Bare Earth Connection

Purpose: Establishing foundational safety, sensory awareness, and present-moment connection.

Time: 10 minutes

Focus: ***Learning***

This grounding practice invites your client to connect directly with the earth using bare feet or hands. Through stillness, breath, and tactile awareness, the client strengthens somatic presence and nervous system regulation while beginning to recognize nature as a supportive co-regulator.

Therapist Preparation:

- **Prepare for Comfort and Choice:** Ensure your client feels safe and physically comfortable. Offer the option of using bare feet or hands depending on temperature, terrain, and personal preference.
- **Site Selection:** Choose a quiet, natural space with soft, clean ground that allows for safe contact with the earth while standing or sitting.

Client Engagement Steps:

1. **Set Intentions:**
- **Offer the frame:** "This practice is about making direct contact with the earth. When we touch the ground with bare skin, we're not just noticing what's around us—we're sensing from within. Let this be a quiet moment of presence, curiosity, and connection."

2. **Invite Engagement:**
- Invite your client to remove their shoes and socks if comfortable. If not, encourage them to place their bare hands on the ground instead.
- Support them in choosing a seated or standing position where they feel grounded and supported.
- Guide them to gently close their eyes and begin slow, conscious breathing: "Breathe in slowly—let your belly rise, then your ribs. Exhale gently. Continue at your own rhythm."
- Invite attention to the sensations at the point of contact: "Notice the texture, temperature, or pressure. What messages is your body receiving through this contact?"
- Allow a few moments of silence for continued sensory observation and internal noticing.

3. **Close the Practice:** Invite your client to take a final deep breath, return attention to the shared space, and put on their footwear when ready.

Clinical Framing & Ongoing Practice

- Encourages nervous system regulation through tactile grounding.
- Builds interoceptive awareness and present-moment focus.
- Supports somatic safety and readiness for deeper work.
- Can be used as a recurring regulation tool or opening practice in future sessions.

Optional Psychoeducation

Offer insight on the physiological effects of earth contact:
"Our hands and feet are rich with sensory receptors. When they touch the earth, our brains often release calming chemicals—like dopamine and serotonin—and activate the parasympathetic nervous system. This is one reason why even short moments of contact with nature can feel so settling."

©2026 Integrating Nature Mental Health Counseling, PLLC. All Rights Reserved

SESSION 3 - **ACTIVITIES**

CATEGORY	Introductory	Integrative	Embodied

Activity 3:2 Shelter Building – Getting Your House in Order

Purpose: Applying personal insight through hands-on engagement and symbolic connection with the natural world.

Time: 40 minutes

Focus: ***Applying***

This activity invites your client to construct a simple natural shelter as a metaphor for the emotional and practical process of 'getting your house in order.' Through physical engagement, reflection, and meaning-making, your client explores themes of effort, support, impermanence, organization, and self-maintenance in a grounded, relational way.

Client Engagement Steps:

1. **Set Intentions:**

- **Offer the frame:** "Today, we'll build a small, 1-person shelter using only what we find here in nature. The process will serve as a metaphor for what it means to get your personal 'house' in order—emotionally, mentally, and physically. As you work, pay attention to what comes up for you internally."

2. **Begin with Guided Reflection:**

- Invite your client to consider the following questions before beginning: "Will what we build today last forever?" and "Will it stay the same until next week?" and "Will it ever need repairing?" **Tip**: *These questions apply not just to the structure your client is building, but also to the emotional and relational structures they live in every day.*

3. **Introduce Materials & Building Process:** Assist your client in gathering and placing the following materials for a 1-person shelter:

- One straight, dry, sturdy 'spine' branch, roughly 4-5in in diameter and 1ft taller than your client's height, should be placed with its butt end against the base of a large, sturdy tree.
- Two 'Y-shaped' branches about 4ft in length should support the to end of the spine branch as it rests in the overlapping crooks of each Y. The bases of each Y-stick should be jammed into the ground at 45° angles away from the peak of the spine, raising it to 3ft.
- The top, 'lifted' end of the spine branch, supported by the Y-sticks, should now have created a triangular 'opening' for the shelter.
- Several straight, dry sticks to form the 'ribs' of the structure (varying in height from 4ft at the opening end to 1ft at the base end by the tree/ground) should be placed against the spine. Remember to stabilize the ribs by sticking them into the ground at an angle, aligning with the bases of the Y-sticks at the opening of the shelter and narrowing their angles of alignment all the way back to the base of the tree. **In this way, your client will essentially be creating a shelter that appears to be a human-sized, A-frame, symmetrical prism; wider on the open end and narrower at the closed end.*
- Several thin, long, flexible branches for weaving between the ribs to form a net-like layer for the roof of the shelter.
- Leaves, bark, or debris for camouflage and coverage to pile (at least 1ft thick) on top of the branch netting until all spaces are filled and no light is able to shine through from the roof to the shelter floor.

Encourage full engagement with the materials—pulling, arranging, and weaving intuitively without a strict plan. Allow 40 minutes for the build.

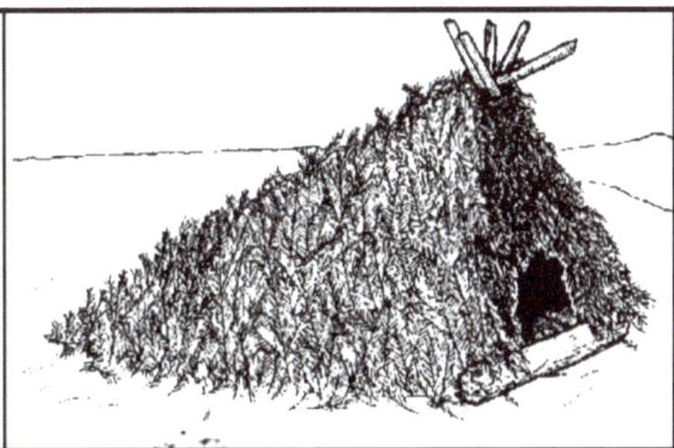

©2026 Integrating Nature Mental Health Counseling, PLLC. All Rights Reserved

SESSION 3 - **ACTIVITIES**

CATEGORY	Introductory	Integrative	Embodied

Activity 3:2 Shelter Building – Getting Your House in Order (Cont'd)

4. **Processing Metaphor in Construction:**
- Reflect on emotional responses to trial and error, moments of frustration, resourcefulness, or decision-making.
- Draw gentle attention to metaphors: "What are you holding together?" "Where does the structure fragile or stable?"

5. **Transition to Debrief Within the Process:** Once the shelter is complete (or as the process naturally slows), invite your client to sit near it and reflect on their experience.

Facilitator prompts:
- "How did the process of building reflect your own life or inner world?"
- "In what ways did this relate to the idea of 'getting your house in order'?"
- "What parts of this felt easy, and what felt challenging?"
- "What kind of maintenance would this shelter need over time—and how does that mirror your own care needs?"

Key themes to explore:
- Thought, effort, and adaptability are required to build something meaningful.
- Personal growth and stability take ongoing maintenance.
- Imperfection and impermanence are part of every structure—natural or emotional.

Activity 3:3 Grounding Practice – Focusing Attention Inward

Purpose: Internalizing presence through somatic awareness and mindful attention to balance and bodily communication.

Time: 10 minutes

Focus: ***Becoming***

This standing mindfulness practice invites your client to develop subtle somatic awareness by focusing on the body's natural balancing movements.
Through breath, stillness, and silence, the client attunes to the quiet exchange between mind and body—cultivating deeper self-regulation, internal presence, and intuitive embodiment.

Therapist Preparation :

- **Model the Practice:** Be prepared to demonstrate the stance and breathing rhythm alongside your client. Stand with feet slightly apart, arms relaxed at your sides, and a soft gaze toward the ground. Practice holding space silently and comfortably.
- **Prepare the Setting:** Choose a level, natural area free of distractions, where your client can stand comfortably. A quiet, shaded spot works well to support stillness and inward focus.

My notes or thoughts for implementing this session:

©2026 Integrating Nature Mental Health Counseling, PLLC. All Rights Reserved

SESSION 3 - **ACTIVITIES**

CATEGORY	Introductory	Integrative	Embodied

Activity 3:3 Grounding Practice – Focusing Attention Inward (Continued)

Client Engagement Steps:

1. **Set Intentions:**

- **Offer the frame:** "This is a grounding practice that helps bring awareness to the subtle ways in which your body and mind communicate—especially in moments of stillness. We're going to focus your attention inward, using breath and balance as a doorway into presence."

2. **Guide the Practice:**

- Invite your client to stand with their feet slightly apart and arms relaxed at their sides.
- Ask them to find a spot on the ground about 3ft in front of them and gently rest their gaze there.
- Model a relaxed stance and slow, even breathing (four counts in, four counts out).

Offer the Prompts:

- "Begin to notice the subtle shifts your body makes as it balances."
- "Are you swaying front to back, side to side? What small adjustments are happening in your torso, feet, or arms?"
- "These tiny movements are always happening—even when you aren't aware of them."

3. **Continue:**

- "Now, bring your attention to how your mind is tracking this balance."
- "Notice how your senses and body are attuning together in real-time."
- "This quiet communication is constant, even when we don't notice it."

4. **Hold Silence:** Let your client stand quietly for 1–2 minutes. Remain present with them while they observe their own inner process.

5. **Close the Practice:** Gently invite your client to take one final breath and return to a seated position beside you. Use the suggested prompt: "When you feel ready, have a seat and take a moment to notice what that experience was like."

Clinical Framing & Ongoing Practice

- Strengthens interoceptive awareness and subtle body-mind attunement.
- Encourages nervous system regulation through grounding and breath.
- Helps build embodied resilience by developing tolerance for stillness and inward focus.
- Can be used as a centering tool to begin or close future sessions.

My notes or thoughts for implementing this session:

©2026 Integrating Nature Mental Health Counseling, PLLC. All Rights Reserved

SESSION 4

RESILIENCE

WHY IS THIS IMPORTANT?
Learning about resilience fosters a growth mindset amid challenges faced by clients and nurtures personal awareness to support the overcoming of life's obstacles.

WHAT YOU NEED TO KNOW IN SUPPORT OF THIS SESSION

WHAT ARE THE BENEFITS OF PRACTICING RESILIENCE?

- Lowers the risk of stress-related physical illness.
- Reduces anxiety and depression.
- Creates stronger social ties.
- Promotes greater longevity.

HOW DOES CORE CALM INCORPORATE RESILIENCE INTO NATURE-BASED THERAPY?

Core Calm incorporates resilience by helping clients build a sense of purpose and supportive relationships, engaging in existing therapy methods like CBT, ACT, and NBT. Being in nature, even for a few hours, causes us to adapt our functions and focus. Our senses are activated, our body must maintain stasis, and we are aware and strengthened by other life around us.

WHAT IS RESILIENCE?

Resilience is the capacity to bounce back and adapt amid challenges by maintaining positivity, problem-solving, and seeking support. Cultivating resilience empowers individuals to navigate tough situations effectively, emerging stronger as a result.

"Resilience is the process and outcome of successfully adapting to difficult or challenging life experiences, especially through mental, emotional, and behavioral flexibility and adjustment to external and internal demands."

"Psychological research demonstrates that the resources and skills associated with resilience can be cultivated and practiced."

American Psychological Association

©2026 Integrating Nature Mental Health Counseling, PLLC. All Rights Reserved

TREATMENT GOAL

After completing this session, the client will be able to gain insight into personal challenges and adapt a flexible mindset via strengthening skills in communication, social engagement, emotional regulation, spirituality, creative investigation, and reflective practices.

GOAL OF THE SESSION

Our goal for this session is to identify resilience in both personal and natural settings.

- The client can identify examples of resilience in nature when they witness animals, plants, and trees coping during tough times, overcoming obstacles, and forming connections. (i.e. saplings grow, bend and stretch in strange ways just to access sunlight).
- The client will acknowledge life's challenges and adapt skills of resilience that mimic examples in nature
- The client will understand that resilience not only means connections to other people, but spiritual connections, mindfulness, or connections to animals, plants, or the earth itself.

©2026 Integrating Nature Mental Health Counseling, PLLC. All Rights Reserved

SESSION 4 - ACTIVITIES

CATEGORY	Introductory	Integrative	Embodied

Activity 4:1 Nature's Resilience Walk – Introduction to Adaptation

Purpose: Introducing the concept of resilience by observing natural adaptations in the environment.

Time: 15 minutes

Focus: ***Learning***

This activity invites your client to explore resilience by taking a mindful walk in nature, paying attention to signs of adaptation and survival. Through direct experience and guided observation, your client learns foundational ideas about resilience as seen in the natural world and begins to connect these concepts to their own lives.

Therapist Preparation:

- **Choose a Diverse Natural Setting:** Select a safe outdoor location with visible examples of natural adaptation, such as plants growing through cracks, trees shaped by wind, or animals' tracks.
- **Prepare Observational Prompts:** Develop simple questions to help the client notice resilience in nature during the walk.

Client Engagement Steps:

1. **Set Intentions:**
- **Offer the frame:** "Resilience means adapting and continuing to grow even when faced with challenges. During this walk, we'll look for ways that plants, trees, and animals show resilience in their environment."

2. **Guide the Practice:**
- Invite your client to walk quietly for 10–15 minutes in the natural setting.
- Encourage them to observe closely and notice examples of nature's resilience, such as:
  - Plants growing in unexpected places
  - Trees bending but not breaking in the wind
  - Signs of regrowth after disturbance (fallen branches, new shoots)
- Pause occasionally to ask them to reflect aloud on what they see:
  - "What adaptations help this plant or tree survive?"
  - "How does this example of resilience remind you of ways you've coped or adapted?"

3. **Silent Reflection:**
  - After the walk, hold 2–3 minutes of silence to journal observations by offering the prompts such as:
  - "What examples of resilience did you notice during the walk?"
  - "How do these natural adaptations relate to your own life experiences?"
  - "What new insights about resilience did you learn today?"
  - "How might you apply these ideas to challenges you're facing?"

4. **Close and Transition the Practice:**
- **Offer the following invitation:** "Take a moment to breathe deeply and think about the resilience you've witnessed today in nature. When you're ready, let's reflect on what this might mean for your own ability to adapt and grow."

Clinical Framing & Ongoing Practice

- Introduces resilience as a natural, adaptive process.
- Builds foundational understanding through experiential learning.
- Encourages mindful observation and connection with the environment.
- Lays the groundwork for deeper resilience practices and personal application.

©2026 Integrating Nature Mental Health Counseling, PLLC. All Rights Reserved

SESSION 4 - ACTIVITIES

CATEGORY	Introductory	Integrative	Embodied

Activity 4:2 Natural Resiliency - Building A Web of Support

Purpose: Applying interpersonal and environmental connections to strengthen resilience.

Time: 30 minutes

Focus: ***Applying***

This practice invites your client to explore their personal sources of resilience by engaging with the natural environment. Through the collection of meaningful natural objects and the creation of a physical web made of yarn, the client externalizes their inner support system. This tactile process helps them recognize, honor, and apply their network of resilience in a tangible and embodied way.

Therapist Preparation:

- **Materials:** Ball of colorful yarn or string, tent stakes (sharpened sticks will do)
- **Choose a Setting:** Choose a calm outdoor location or natural setting with access to small, safe-to-collect objects (leaves, stones, twigs, pinecones, etc.). If indoors, provide a small basket of pre-gathered natural objects or invite the client to collect some before the session.

Client Engagement Steps:

1. **Set Intentions:**

- **Offer the frame:** "Resilience isn't something we have to carry alone—it's often held up by the people, places, and practices that support us. Today, we'll gather symbols from the natural world to represent those supports and connect them to build a 'resilience web.' This is a way to see how your sources of strength come together and how you can rely on them."

2. **Guide the Practice:**

- Begin by inviting your client to slowly walk through the area and gather 5–7 small natural objects. Encourage them to do this quietly and intuitively, selecting items that draw their attention or feel meaningful. Offer guidance as needed: "Each object you choose will represent a source of resilience & support in your life—someone who's helped you, a place you go to feel safe, or a practice that brings you calm or strength."
- Engage somatic and symbolic awareness by connecting the client's inner experience with their external environment using the following prompt: "Notice textures, shapes, colors—anything that feels right to you."

3. **Place the Objects with Intention:**

- After gathering, invite the client to place each object spread 3-5 ft apart in front of them. As they place each item, ask them to name or reflect on what type of resilience it represents. For example:
    - A stone might represent a dependable friend.
    - A leaf might symbolize growth through therapy.
    - A curved twig might reflect flexibility or change.

4. **Create the Yarn Web:**

- Offer the client a ball of yarn and the stakes. Instruct them to begin by placing the stakes in the ground next to their objects. Then tie or pin the yarn to the stakes. *Make sure the yarn is stretched back and forth among the objects to connect them in a web-like structure. As they build, ask reflective questions to deepen awareness:
    - "What do you notice about how you have grown to be resilience as these supports begin to connect?"
    - "Where do you feel strength in this web?"
    - "What part of your life feels most held or most vulnerable right now?"

This process externalizes the client's support system, showing visually how seemingly separate sources of resilience are interconnected.

©2026 Integrating Nature Mental Health Counseling, PLLC. All Rights Reserved

SESSION 4 - ACTIVITIES

CATEGORY	Introductory	Integrative	Embodied

Activity 4:2 Natural Resiliency - Building A Web of Support (Continued)

5. **Journaling or Verbal Reflection:**

- After the web is complete, invite the client to reflect through journaling or dialogue. Offer prompts such as:
  - "What does this web say about how you are supported?"
  - "What connections feel strong? Are there any you want to strengthen?"
  - "How can you actively rely on or reach out to these supports when life feels overwhelming?"
  - "What might you add to this web in the future?"

Clinical Framing & Ongoing Practice

- Integrates personal, relational, and environmental supports into a unified visual metaphor.
- Applies resilience concepts through sensory engagement and symbolic meaning-making.
- Offers a grounding, hands-on intervention that can be revisited and adapted as resilience evolves.
- Encourages clients to build habits of identifying, reaching for, and nurturing sources of strength.

Activity 4:3 Rooted Stance – Embodying Inner Strength

Purpose: Cultivating stability and strength through grounded posture and breath.

Time: 10 minutes

Focus: ***Becoming***

This practice invites your client to embody the feeling of being rooted and strong by exploring their connection to the ground beneath them. Through mindful posture, breath, and somatic awareness, the client begins to become more attuned to their own internal resilience, developing a felt sense of steadiness, strength, and rooted presence even amidst inner or outer turbulence.

Therapist Preparation:

- **Choose a Grounded Setting:** Select a quiet natural area with firm ground—dirt, grass, or a flat patch of earth where the client can stand barefoot or in grounded footwear. Shaded, private spots work best to support inward focus.
- **Model the Practice:** Be prepared to demonstrate the stance yourself. Stand with feet hip-width apart, knees slightly bent, arms relaxed at your sides, and spine lengthened. Model calm breath and presence.

Client Engagement Steps:

1. **Set Intentions:**

- **Offer the frame:** "Like a tree, we all have the capacity to root ourselves—to stand firm even when the world around us feels uncertain. Today, we'll practice becoming grounded through our breath and body, so you can begin to feel the strength you already carry within."

2. **Guide the Practice:**

- **Find Stability:** Invite your client to stand with feet hip-width apart, encouraging them to feel the contact between their feet and the earth. If they feel comfortable, they can close their eyes or soften their gaze.
  - "Notice the shape of the ground beneath you. Let your weight drop fully into your feet."

©2026 Integrating Nature Mental Health Counseling, PLLC. All Rights Reserved

SESSION 4 - **ACTIVITIES**

CATEGORY	Introductory	Integrative	Embodied

Activity 4:3 Rooted Stance – Embodying Inner Strength (Continued)

- **Engage Somatic Awareness: Prompt gentle movements to increase presence:**
  - "Gently sway from side to side, forward and back—like a tree adjusting to wind."
  - "Now come to stillness, letting your body find its natural balance point."
  - "Feel your legs holding you, your spine stacking, your breath moving through you."

- **Introduce Root Imagery:** Invite them to imagine roots growing from the soles of their feet, down into the earth.
  - **"**With each inhale, draw in strength from the ground. With each exhale, send your roots deeper. Even if the wind blows, a tree with deep roots remains standing."

- **Breathe into the Stance:** Guide slow, rhythmic breathing (e.g., 4-count inhale, 6-count exhale)
  - "With each breath, you are practicing presence. Practicing strength. Practicing trust in your own capacity to stay upright."

- **Silent Integration:** Hold 1–2 minutes of silence for the client to stand in their rooted stance and feel their body's quiet strength.

- **Close the Practice:** Invite a transition back: "Take one final breath here. Begin to gently shift your weight, maybe wiggle your toes or roll your shoulders. When you're ready, step back from the stance—and notice how you carry that rooted feeling with you."

- **Reflection Prompts (Verbal or Journaling):**
  - "What did you notice in your body during the rooted stance?"
  - "What helped you feel steadier or stronger?"
  - "In what moments in life do you most need this feeling of rootedness?"
  - "What does it mean to become someone who can hold steady even in stress?"

Clinical Framing & Ongoing Practice

- Anchors resilience in a felt, bodily experience rather than just cognitive understanding.
- Develops self-trust through embodied awareness of balance and support.
- Encourages 'becoming' resilient by reinforcing strength through repetition and presence.
- Offers a portable, somatic tool that clients can use when emotionally dysregulated or overwhelmed.

My notes or thoughts for implementing this session:

©2026 Integrating Nature Mental Health Counseling, PLLC. All Rights Reserved

SESSION 5

DISTRESS TOLERANCE

WHY IS THIS IMPORTANT?
Distress tolerance equips your client to manage intense emotions and urges without resorting to harmful behaviors or impulsive decisions. These skills help your client navigate crises, tolerate painful emotions, and build resilience for long-term well-being.

WHAT YOU NEED TO KNOW IN SUPPORT OF THIS SESSION

WHAT ARE THE BENEFITS OF PRACTICING DISTRESS TOLERANCE?

- Improves emotional regulation and resilience.
- Reduces impulsive behavior and strengthens problem-solving skills.
- Enhances relationships and decreases symptoms of anxiety and depression.

HOW DOES CORE CALM INCORPORATE DISTRESS TOLERANCE INTO NATURE-BASED THERAPY?

Through integrating the principles of ACT, clients learn to engage with stress using healthy coping mechanisms such as acknowledgment and acceptance. Ecotherapy activities challenge and stimulate us via affective, kinesthetic, and cognitive interaction.

WHAT IS DISTRESS TOLERANCE?

Distress tolerance refers to the ability to endure emotional discomfort without resorting to harmful or negative coping mechanisms. In psychology research, it is a crucial aspect in understanding and treating anxiety disorders like posttraumatic stress disorder (PTSD), panic disorder, obsessive-compulsive disorder (OCD), and generalized anxiety disorder (GAD).

Studies show that low distress tolerance is linked to heightened anxiety and symptom development.

Interventions such as cognitive-behavioral therapies (CBT) and mindfulness aim to enhance distress tolerance, offering promising avenues for treatment.

©2026 Integrating Nature Mental Health Counseling, PLLC. All Rights Reserved

TREATMENT GOAL

After completing this session, the client will be equipped with enhanced distress tolerance by integrating ACT principles and promoting feelings of safety in a natural setting. Specifically, the client will learn to manage emotional dysregulation by engaging with distress, practicing acceptance strategies, fostering resilience, and developing positive coping skills.

GOAL OF THE SESSION

Our goal for this session is to introduce the client to ACT and radical acceptance.

- The client will be able to define radical acceptance as *not equal to* forgiveness or permission but rather acknowledgment of the reality of the situation (i.e. one's life is not defined by their experiences but by their choices in responding to them).
- The client will be able to identify the power of acceptance.
- The client will practice acknowledging and embracing their reality as it stands rather than resisting or attempting to alter it.
- The client will develop a practice of radical acceptance to alleviate unnecessary suffering from negative thoughts, behaviors and emotions.

©2026 Integrating Nature Mental Health Counseling, PLLC. All Rights Reserved

SESSION 5 - ACTIVITIES

CATEGORY	Introductory	Integrative	Embodied

Activity 5:1 Radical Acceptance – Practicing Distress Tolerance

Purpose: Building awareness of emotional experiences and distress tolerance through metaphor, mindfulness, and ACT-based reflection.

Time: 15 minutes

Focus: ***Learning***

This activity introduces your client to distress tolerance with the suggested poem "The Guest House" by Rumi, as a metaphor for emotional acceptance. Guided discussion and reflection help the client explore Acceptance and Commitment Therapy (ACT) principles, specifically radical acceptance, and how pausing to acknowledge reality can reduce suffering and increase psychological flexibility.

Therapist Preparation:

- **Bring the Poem:** Print or bring a copy of "The Guest House" by Rumi to read aloud. Familiarize yourself with the key message so you can guide interpretation.
- **Choose the Setting:** Select a quiet, calming natural area—such as near a tree, fire circle, or creek—where your client can sit comfortably and reflect without distraction.

Client Engagement Steps:

1. **Set Intentions:**

- **Offer the frame:** "Today, we'll explore how we can become more open to our emotions, especially the difficult ones. This is a foundational skill in distress tolerance. We'll begin by hearing a poem and then reflect on how its message connects to how we handle life's challenges."

2. **Guide the Practice:**

Part A – Suggested Reading & Reflection: "The Guest House" by Rumi (5 minutes)

- Invite your client to sit comfortably and take a few grounding breaths.
- Read the poem slowly and clearly, after which, guide a brief discussion with prompts such as:
  - "What stands out to you in this poem?"
  - "How does this idea of 'welcoming each emotion as a guest' relate to how you experience distress?"
  - "What's hard about treating difficult emotions with this kind of openness?"
- Reinforce that the poem models emotional acceptance—not resistance—as a path to healing.

Part B – Practice Imagery Through ACT & Radical Acceptance (10 minutes)

- Connect the key takeaways from the discussion of the poem to the idea of radical acceptance using the suggested prompt:
  - "Let's look at how we can take this idea into everyday life; Imagine you have a really important appointment and just before you plan to leave, you walk to your car and notice a flat tire."
- Ask your client to describe what thoughts and emotions might show up.
- Reflect together on how those thoughts might shape reactions in a stepwise fashion:
  - "Would you feel anxious? Angry? Frustrated?"
  - "How might those feelings affect your behavior? Explain your response in four steps."

©2026 Integrating Nature Mental Health Counseling, PLLC. All Rights Reserved

SESSION 5 - **ACTIVITIES**

CATEGORY	Introductory	Integrative	Embodied

Activity 5:1 Radical Acceptance – Practicing Distress Tolerance (Continued)

- Introduce ACT's concept of radical acceptance:
  - "Rather than wishing the tire wasn't flat, we acknowledge that it is. That doesn't mean we like it—but we accept reality so we can move forward."
- It is important to clarify that radical acceptance is not approval or passivity—it is naming what is true so we can respond more skillfully. This is an act that grants spaciousness around processing the situation and allows for effective decision-making.
- Return to the poem as a bridge and ask your client to reimagine an emotionally regulated approach to the problem of the flat tire, again using a stepwise thought process:
  - "Like the poem, radical acceptance invites us to welcome our emotional responses without pushing them away. Every thought or feeling is a visitor. Explain what might shift for you if you practiced treating those "visitors" with less resistance? Frame your new response, again using only four steps."

Clinical Framing & Ongoing Practice

- Introduces distress tolerance by combining metaphor (poetry) with real-life scenarios.
- Reinforces ACT principles of emotional acceptance, present-moment awareness, and choice.
- Helps normalize emotional discomfort and reduce judgment toward negative thoughts and feelings.
- Supports future work on resilience, mindfulness, and values-based action.

My notes or thoughts for implementing this session:

©2026 Integrating Nature Mental Health Counseling, PLLC. All Rights Reserved

Radical Acceptance Worksheet

Objective: Assess your ACT skills in a specific situation so that you are more prepared to accept.

1. Situation

What happened?
(Describe the event or circumstance you are struggling to accept.)

2. My Initial Reactions

Thoughts:
(What thoughts came up automatically?)

Feelings:
(What emotions am I feeling? Rate intensity of each from 0–10)

Urges/Behaviors:
(What did I want to do or what did I do?)

3. Practicing Radical Acceptance

What's out of my control?

What can I choose to accept (even if I don't like it)?

ACT Skill Check:

- ☐ Defusion (stepping back from thoughts)
- ☐ Present-moment awareness
- ☐ Willingness/Acceptance
- ☐ Values focus
- ☐ Committed action

4. What Acceptance Looks Like

If I accepted this fully, I would...
(Write what you would do if you stopped fighting reality.)

©2026 Integrating Nature Mental Health Counseling, PLLC. All Rights Reserved

Radical Acceptance Worksheet Cont'd.

ACT skill

5. What Acceptance Feels Like
What does acceptance feel like in my body? (Notice any sensations or changes.)

6. Moving Forward
One small action I can take that aligns with my values:
Self-compassion statement: (Example: "This is hard, and I can handle it.")

REMINDER

Tolerating distressing moments becomes easier with acceptance - this does not mean approval, but rather acknowledgment. It means choosing to accept reality so you can focus your energy on what matters most, commitment to finding resolution.

UNDERSTANDING HUMAN NATURE & PSYCHOLOGICAL DISTRESS

By linking **psychological difficulties** with **adaptive responses for survival**, we begin to notice where our **perspectives may be distorted**. With this approach, we understand our human nature and teach ourselves that our conditioned reactions are not permanent. We can learn to change the way we think, feel and behave.

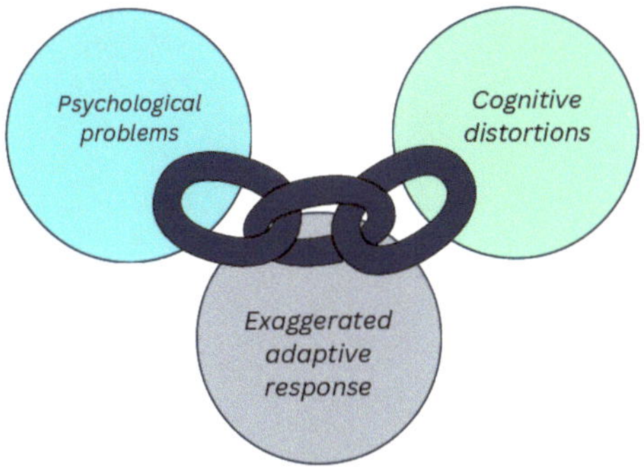

©2026 Integrating Nature Mental Health Counseling, PLLC. All Rights Reserved

Becoming Psychologically Flexible

ACT skill

Psychological flexibility is the ability to adapt to life's difficulties while remaining true to one's values. This skill consists of six key components, which are illustrated below. Developing these traits leads to greater resilience, emotional tolerance, and overall well-being.

Read on to learn about these traits. Use the action steps to become more psychologically flexible and enjoy its many benefits. Practice regularly for the best results.

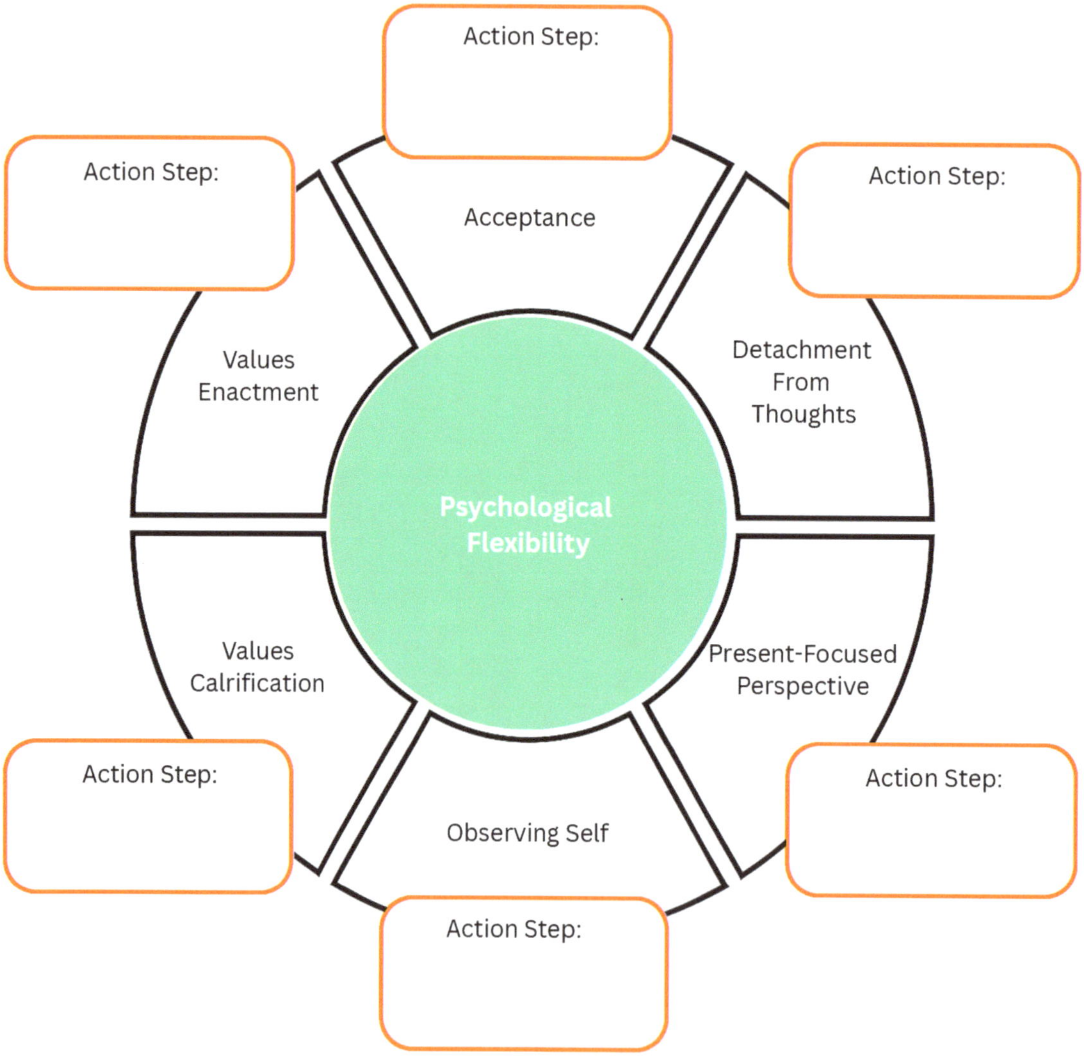

My notes or thoughts for implementing this activity:

©2026 Integrating Nature Mental Health Counseling, PLLC. All Rights Reserved

SESSION 5 - **ACTIVITIES**

CATEGORY	Introductory	Integrative	Embodied

Activity 5:2 The Trigger Tree Challenge – Practicing Distress Tolerance Through Acceptance

Purpose: Applying acceptance-based practices to build emotional resilience and expand distress tolerance.

Time: 35 minutes

Focus: ***Applying***

This experiential activity challenges your client to face a distressing memory through the symbolic use of a tree in nature. By practicing psychological acceptance rather than resistance, your client engages directly with discomfort while developing emotional regulation and cognitive flexibility. The tree becomes a metaphor for the immovability of the past, and the body becomes the vehicle for practicing a different relationship to suffering.

Therapist Preparation:

- **Choose the Setting:** Identify a wooded or open natural area with visible trees that are spaced far enough apart for privacy, but still within safe sight distance. Ideally, the space allows quiet immersion while remaining grounded within the therapeutic container.
- **Prepare Client for Emotional Intensity:** Briefly acknowledge that this is a challenging exercise and that it's okay if the client chooses to stop or take space at any time. Emphasize choice and emotional safety throughout.

Client Engagement Steps:

1. **Set Intentions:**

- **Offer the frame:** "Today's activity will help us explore how our thoughts and emotions interact when we recall something difficult. You'll work with a tree as a symbol of that experience—not to change it, but to notice your reaction to it and practice meeting it differently."

2. **Guided Instructions (30 Minutes Total)**

- **Tree Selection (3–5 minutes):** Invite your client to walk slowly and intuitively choose a tree that feels "right" for this activity. The tree trunk diameter should be no smaller than 8-12 inches (for sturdiness). Ask them to stand about 15 feet away from the trunk once selected.

- **Memory Visualization (3–5 minutes):** Instruct your client to visualize the tree as if it had a screen on it. On that screen, they will privately replay a challenging event from any time in their life. They are not expected to share it—only to recall it and allow the associated thoughts and feelings to arise.

- **Approach with Awareness (5 minutes):**
  - Guide your client to begin walking slowly toward the tree, one step at a time. As they get closer, suggest they notice how the memory becomes more vivid, emotionally and physically.
  - Encourage them to observe their internal state with each step (it is suggested that you use a firm but compassionate tone throughout this process).

- **Physical Contact & Resistance (5 minutes):**
  - Once at the tree, invite your client to place both hands on the trunk.
  - Begin with a gentle push. Notice how it feels to try to move the tree.
  - Increase the pressure, as if trying to push the tree—and the memory—away completely (state your instructions firmly to invoke a bit more emotion).
  - Allow them to notice the effort, frustration, and futility of resisting something that cannot be changed (state your instructions with increasing firmness).

©2026 Integrating Nature Mental Health Counseling, PLLC. All Rights Reserved

SESSION 5 - **ACTIVITIES**

CATEGORY	Introductory	Integrative	Embodied

Activity 5:2 The Trigger Tree Challenge – Practicing Distress Tolerance Through Acceptance (Continued)

- **Release & Reframe (3–5 minutes):**
  - With a gentle voice, ask your client to drop their hands, step back from the tree, and take three deep breaths. Then step to one side and view the tree and the forest around them from a different angle.
  - Invite them to look beyond the tree, to the space and forest around them, noticing what else exists beyond the singular focus of their distress.

- **Silent Reflection (3–5 minutes):** Allow a moment of silence for your client to take in the full experience, view all the other trees in the first around them in the context of other, good memories or experiences and, consider what they've been missing while they have been hyper focused on this one negative, unchangeable experience/memory. You may say: "Once we stop pushing against the things we cannot change, we create space and redirect energy to see what other good exists in our lives, what else is possible. Acceptance doesn't mean approval—it means we stop wasting our energy on battles we can't win."

3. **Closing Integration**

- Invite your client to spend 2-3 minutes processing this experience on their own; they may want to return to a seated space (e.g., a grounding location) to pace slowly. *Remind them to utilize silent breathwork and reflection.
- Simply affirm your client's effort here and remind them to honor their dedication: "This kind of work takes courage. Even if it doesn't feel like resolution right away, the act of showing up and being with your experience builds strength."
- If you assess that your client is open to receiving insight, offer a thoughtful prompt such as: "Building tolerance for distressing experiences or memories is a natural part of and order of things in nature. Where there is chaos, life finds a balance through resilience."

Clinical Framing & Ongoing Practice

- Reinforces distress tolerance through active acceptance of discomfort.
- Enhances the client's capacity for emotional regulation and cognitive flexibility.
- Builds an embodied understanding of the futility of resistance and the freedom of acknowledgment.
- Can be revisited as a touchpoint for working with grief, trauma, or shame.
- Teaches clients to recognize that healing includes looking beyond the distress.

My notes or thoughts for implementing this session:

©2026 Integrating Nature Mental Health Counseling, PLLC. All Rights Reserved

SESSION 5 - ACTIVITIES

CATEGORY	Introductory	Integrative	Embodied

Activity 5:3 Internal Weather Report – Emotional Awareness Through Metaphor and Relaxation

Purpose: Supporting emotional regulation through metaphor, breath, and parasympathetic activation.

Time: 10 minutes

Focus: ***Becoming***

This practice engages the parasympathetic nervous system by encouraging creative expression, relational presence, and mindful awareness of internal states. Using nature-based metaphors like weather patterns, your client explores their emotional experience through imagery and embodied reflection, promoting increased distress tolerance and emotional flexibility.

Therapist Preparation:

- **Choose the Setting:** Select a quiet, sheltered space in nature with limited sensory distractions. A small clearing, grove, or shaded spot is ideal for grounding and relaxation.
- **Set the Tone:** Invite your client into a slower pace by gently transitioning from any previous activity into this quieter, inward-focused experience.

Client Engagement Steps:

1. **Set Intentions:**
- **Offer the frame:** "Let's take a few minutes to tune in to what's going on inside. We'll use something called an 'internal weather report' to check in with how you're feeling—without judgment—just observation."

2. **Guide the Practice:**
- **Grounding & Orientation:** Invite your client to sit or stand in a comfortable position. Encourage them to feel the ground beneath their feet and to take a few slow, intentional breaths. As they breathe, suggest that they begin to notice their internal state, just like noticing the weather outside.
- **Internal Weather Check-In:** Ask your client to quietly reflect on how their emotional landscape might be described as weather.
  - Are they feeling cloudy? Calm and clear? Stormy? Foggy?
  - Has their "weather" changed throughout the day or activity?
  - Encourage them to describe their internal experience creatively and with curiosity. For example: "I felt sunny this morning, but now there's a low-pressure system moving in—some tension behind my eyes and a foggy feeling in my chest."

- **Introduce Root Imagery:** Invite them to imagine roots growing from the soles of their feet, down into the earth.
  - "With each inhale, draw in strength from the ground. With each exhale, send your roots deeper. Even if the wind blows, a tree with deep roots remains standing."

- **Verbal Sharing & Embodiment:** If comfortable, invite your client to speak their internal weather report aloud. Support them in anchoring their awareness in the body by gently asking:
  - "Where in your body do you feel that weather showing up?"
  - "What does that sensation remind you of in nature?"

- **Closing the Practice:** Invite one final slow breath. Acknowledge the effort it takes to tune inward and stay present with internal states. Gently return focus to the shared space.

©2026 Integrating Nature Mental Health Counseling, PLLC. All Rights Reserved

SESSION 5 - **ACTIVITIES**

CATEGORY	Introductory	Integrative	Embodied

Activity 5:3 Internal Weather Report – Emotional Awareness Through Metaphor and Relaxation (Cont'd)

3. **Integration & Reflection:**

- Offer a soft reflection to end the practice: "Sometimes just naming how we feel—without needing to change it—can help us shift out of survival mode. Like the weather, our emotions change. And like the natural world, we have the ability to observe those changes without getting swept away by them."
- Encourage your client to return to this metaphor when emotions feel intense or hard to name.

Clinical Framing & Ongoing Practice

- Enhances interoceptive awareness and nonjudgmental emotional tracking.
- Encourages creative expression and symbolic thinking in distressing moments.
- Supports nervous system regulation through breath, imagery, and present-moment fous.
- Reinforces the idea that emotions—like weather—are temporary, natural, and movable.

My notes or thoughts for implementing this session:

©2026 Integrating Nature Mental Health Counseling, PLLC. All Rights Reserved

SESSION 6

ADVANCED MINDFULNESS

WHY IS THIS IMPORTANT?

Advanced mindfulness, immersed in an natural therapeutic setting, helps clients cultivate deeper self-awareness, emotional regulation, and resilience, empowering them to navigate complex psychological challenges with greater insight and stability.

WHAT YOU NEED TO KNOW IN SUPPORT OF THIS SESSION

WHAT ARE THE BENEFITS OF PRACTICING ADVANCED MINDFULNESS?

- Reduces stress.
- Increases self-awareness.
- Strengthens emotional regulation.
- Improves relationships.
- Enhances well-being and quality of life.

HOW DOES CORE CALM INCORPORATE ADVANCED MINDFULNESS INTO NATURE-BASED THERAPY?

Advanced mindfulness expands awareness beyond the self to include our connection with the natural world. By attending to the places we inhabit, we gain insight into ourselves, our communities, and our shared history. This perspective, known as Terrapsychology, highlights the role of place in shaping human experience.

Coined by Craig Chalquist, PhD, Terrapsychology is defined as "the relationship between Psyche and Place; a study of how terrain, place, element, and natural process show up in human psychology, endeavor, and story, including myth and legend. It begins with the premise that we are not separate from the sites where we live and work."

WHAT IS ADVANCED MINDFULNESS?

Mindfulness is about being present without judgment, fostering awareness of thoughts and feelings. It promotes calmness and clarity by accepting experiences without reacting impulsively or perseverating. Regular practice, such as meditation, *enhances* emotional regulation and mental resilience.

"Mindfulness is awareness of one's internal states and surroundings. Mindfulness can help people avoid destructive or automatic habits and responses by learning to observe their automatic thoughts, emotions, in the present moment without judging or reacting to them.

Mindfulness is used in several therapeutic interventions, including mindfulness-based cognitive behavior therapy, mindfulness-based stress reduction, and mindfulness meditation."

American Psychological Association

©2026 Integrating Nature Mental Health Counseling, PLLC. All Rights Reserved

TREATMENT GOAL

After completing this session, the client will be able to expand awareness beyond the self by revisiting nature-based mindfulness that explores awareness of connection between surrounding environment, body (somatic) and emotions to enhance attention and self-regulation.

GOAL OF THE SESSION

Our goal for this session is to deepen mindfulness by fostering awareness of connection to place, nature, and collective experience.

- The client will remember that mindfulness empowers them to return their attention to the present moment, enabling them to live more fully with greater choice, engagement, and presence.
- The client will be called to back to their roots as humans in earth-based cultures, where living mindfully without judgment was inherent.
- The client will learn that advanced mindfulness is considered radical because it departs from traditional mindfulness by prioritizing surface-level reflection on past events and emphasizing objective observation without judgment.

©2026 Integrating Nature Mental Health Counseling, PLLC. All Rights Reserved

SESSION 6 - **ACTIVITIES**

CATEGORY	Introductory	Integrative	Embodied

Activity 6:1 Forest Bathing – Deepening Mindful Awareness Through Nature

Purpose: Introducing advanced mindfulness through immersive sensory presence in a forest environment.

Time: 15 minutes

Focus: ***Learning***

Forest bathing, or Shinrin-yoku, is a mindfulness-based practice that invites deep sensory immersion in a natural setting. Rather than focusing on physical exertion, this practice supports parasympathetic nervous system regulation, emotional awareness, and presence by slowing down and observing the living world *without judgment*. In a 1:1 context, forest bathing serves as an entry point into advanced mindfulness by cultivating a calm, attuned relationship with nature.

Therapist Preparation:

- **Select the Route**: Choose a quiet, scenic path or wooded area with natural variety—trees, textures, light, and sound—to enrich the sensory experience. Prioritize accessibility and calmness.
- **Embodied Modeling:** Move slowly, breathe intentionally, and maintain a quiet presence to help co-regulate your client's pace and awareness.

Client Engagement Steps:

1. **Set Intentions:** Invite your client into a quiet, contemplative walk where they'll explore the natural environment using their senses as a guide. Explain that the goal is not to reach a destination, but to experience presence through the sights, sounds, and sensations of the forest *without judging any observation* – just notice.

2. **Begin the Practice:** Guide your client to begin walking slowly and mindfully. Encourage them to use their breath to anchor attention, and gently direct awareness to things such as:

- Visual textures, colors, and movement in trees and undergrowth
- Natural sounds—wind, birds, insects, crunching leaves
- Scents in the air—bark, pine, damp earth
- Physical sensations—air on the skin, feet on the ground, fingers touching tree bark or leaves

3. **Silent Reflection:** As the walk concludes, invite your client to come to stillness and gently notice what sensations or thoughts remain. They may be guided to speak their name softly into the space, reinforcing their presence and connection.

   Encourage quiet internal reflection through grounding questions such as:
   - "How do I feel connected to this place right now?"
   - "What part of nature is mirroring how I feel inside?"

4. **Closing Integration:** Invite your client to sit or stand quietly and reflect on their experience through journaling. Encourage written observations about their emotional state, physical sensations, or sense of connection to the natural surroundings. Allow these reflections to emerge without pressure to analyze or solve anything. You might ask:
   - "What did you notice about your body, your thoughts, or the world around you?"

- Let this be an open-ended opportunity for your client to notice without judgment and to carry that awareness beyond the session.

©2026 Integrating Nature Mental Health Counseling, PLLC. All Rights Reserved

SESSION 6 - ACTIVITIES

CATEGORY	Introductory	Integrative	Embodied

Activity 6:1 Forest Bathing – Deepening Mindful Awareness Through Nature (Continued)

Clinical Framing & Ongoing Practice

- Supports **nervous system regulation** by activating rest-and-digest states.
- Reinforces **sensory mindfulness** as a skill for managing stress, overwhelm, and cognitive fatigue.
- Encourages nonjudgmental observation and connection with nature as a **co-regulator**.
- Builds capacity for **sustained attention and embodied awareness.**
- Offers an accessible tool that can be practiced independently between sessions.

Activity 6:2 The Golden Question – Mindfulness Without Judgment

Purpose: Applying and personalizing mindfulness skills; deepening the connection between internal experience and the natural world.

Time: 30 minutes

Focus: ***Applying***

This integrative mindfulness activity supports clients in exploring a past experience using present-moment awareness, observation without judgment, and metaphor drawn from the natural world. The "Golden Question" — *What is going on here?* — becomes a tool to reframe stress-inducing events with clarity, neutrality, and grounding. Nature offers a living mirror for acceptance and adaptation, allowing the client to witness and reflect through a lens of nonjudgmental.

Therapist Preparation:

- **Identify a Natural Reflection Spot:** Choose a setting rich with subtle variation—trees with broken limbs, plant life adapting to environmental pressures, or other natural metaphors of resilience and neutrality.
- **Model Nonjudgmental Presence:** Approach the practice with stillness and curiosity, mirroring the tone and pace you wish your client to embody. Be aware of your own body language, tone, and breathing.

Client Engagement Steps:

1. **Introduction and Orientation:** Begin by walking slowly with your client to a quiet spot in nature. Invite your client to sit or stand comfortably in a place where they can observe the natural world, such as a tree adapting to damage, a plant growing toward sunlight, or shifting weather patterns.

- Explain that nature is constantly adapting without judgment. A tree that leans from the wind or bends for light doesn't resist—it simply grows in response.

2. **Observation Without Judgment:** Invite your client to observe a specific element in their surroundings that appears to have shifted, endured, or adapted. Instruct them to focus on this element in nature without interpretation. Just notice what is there—colors, shape, texture, movement. See if you can describe it as factually as possible."

- Once grounded in observation, invite your client to turn attention inward to scan muscles, heartbeat, breath, internal temperature, sensations of pain or calm.

3. **Internal Reflection Using the Golden Question:** Ask your client to recall a mild, recent moment of stress—something manageable that does not activate crisis-level emotion; A difficult conversation, a frustrating delay, or a moment of tension.

©2026 Integrating Nature Mental Health Counseling, PLLC. All Rights Reserved

SESSION 6 - **ACTIVITIES**

CATEGORY	Introductory	Integrative	Embodied

Activity 6:2 The Golden Question – Mindfulness Without Judgment (Continued)

- Guide your client to reflect *generally* on this moment aloud without getting into too much detail or analysis. Instead, they are asked to answer *The Golden Question*: "What is going on here?"
- Support them in distilling their memory into four factual statements—free of interpretation or opinion.
- Encourage your client to notice how it felt in their body at the time, and how it feels now as they are revisiting it.

4. **Metaphorical Integration with Nature:** Invite your client to return their attention to the natural element they were observing earlier. Prompt gentle comparison: "What can this tree/plant/weather pattern teach about facing stress without judgment?"
- Allow your client to name a takeaway or observation that connects their personal experience to the resilience or neutrality modeled in nature.

5. **Self-Compassion and Present Anchoring:** Ask your client what they might say to their past self if they could offer guidance from this grounded, present place. Invite this to be quietly journaled and then spoken aloud.

6. **Closing Integration:** Guide your client to take three slow, deep breaths and name one word to describe their current state. Encourage a final moment of noticing—"What has shifted in their body, mind, or perspective?"
Invite your client to thank the natural space around them, and to recognize its role in supporting reflection and calm.

Clinical Framing & Ongoing Practice

- Strengthens your client's ability to separate fact from interpretation in emotionally charged moments.
- Promotes radical mindfulness by linking nonjudgmental awareness to real-time nervous system regulation.
- Uses nature as a mirror for practicing neutrality, observation, and adaptability.
- Enhances emotional resilience by reinforcing internal safety and clarity under stress.
- Offers a replicable mindfulness tool (The Golden Question) for daily distress tolerance.

Activity 6:3 Embodied Awareness - Stretching Into Stillness

Purpose: Deepening present-moment awareness and sensory embodiment through natural movement and mindful stretching.

Time: 10 minutes

Focus: ***Becoming***

This activity supports advanced mindfulness practice by engaging the body in intuitive stretching while immersed in a natural setting. Through this brief but focused movement sequence, your client is invited to expand their somatic awareness, release tension, and gently explore the interplay between internal experience and the surrounding environment. The aim is to deepen sensory awareness and interoception, while enhancing the client's ability to attend to the present moment without narrative or judgment.

Therapist Preparation:

- **Choose the Setting:** Select an open, quiet natural area with flat ground where the client can stand or sit comfortably—this could include a forest clearing, field edge, lakeshore, or meadow trail. Choose a space where movement can happen without self-consciousness, and where the client has access to soft natural sounds and consistent ground surface.
- **Prepare the Client for Somatic Attention:** Briefly introduce the idea that this practice involves slow, gentle movement rather than formal stretching or performance. Normalize natural pauses, asymmetry, and internal observation.

©2026 Integrating Nature Mental Health Counseling, PLLC. All Rights Reserved

SESSION 6 - ACTIVITIES

CATEGORY	Introductory	Integrative	Embodied

Activity 6:3 Embodied Awareness - Stretching Into Stillness (Continued)

Client Engagement Steps:

1. **Set Intentions:**
- **Offer the frame:** "Today's practice is about tuning in—not trying to stretch 'the right way,' but moving with awareness and allowing nature to help us notice how we feel in the body. We're not here to judge or correct—just to listen."

2. **Guide the Practice:**
- **Grounding & Orientation:** Invite your client to stand or sit in a grounded posture with both feet supported by the earth. Suggest they feel the weight of their body, and gently shift forward and back or side to side until they find balance. Encourage them to breathe slowly, allowing their attention to settle into their feet, legs, hips, and spine. Invite silence as they orient to the surrounding space. Consider the prompt: "What's one word your body might want to move toward today—ease, stretch, stillness?"
- **Exploratory Movement Sequence:** Encourage your client to allow intuitive, slow movement without fixed positions. Allow long pauses between suggestions. Offer the prompt: "As you move, notice: where is there space? Where is there resistance? What wants to release?"

  Suggested movements:
  - Gentle side bends and twists, with arms hanging or lifted like branches.
  - Overhead stretches reaching toward the sky or treetops.
  - Rolling willers, neck, or wrists with curiosity.
  - Stretching down toward the earth, allowing knees to bend.
  - Encourage your client to match their pace to natural rhythms around them—birdsong, wind, distant water. Suggest they pause occasionally to notice sensations without rushing forward.

- **Stillness & Internal Reflection:** Invite the client to return to a neutral posture. Suggest one hand rest on the heart, the other on the belly, or both at the sides. Invite them to notice:
  - What feels different in the body now?
  - Is there a sense of warmth, tingling, or openness?
  - What in the environment mirrors this internal shift?

Allow a few deep breaths in silence before inviting your client to look slowly around the space and re-enter relational presence with you.

3. **Closing Integration:**
- Offer a gentle reflection to affirm the client's effort: "Our bodies carry a lot—sometimes more than we realize. When we slow down and listen, we stretch more than our muscles—we stretch our awareness. And sometimes that's enough."
  - Encourage your client to return to this practice when they feel disconnected from their body or need to ground themselves in the present moment through nature.

My notes or thoughts for implementing this session:

©2026 Integrating Nature Mental Health Counseling, PLLC. All Rights Reserved

SESSION 6 - **ACTIVITIES**

CATEGORY	Introductory	Integrative	Embodied

Activity 6:3 Embodied Awareness - Stretching Into Stillness (Continued)

Clinical Framing & Ongoing Practice

- Enhances interoceptive and sensory awareness in real-time.
- Reinforces present-moment focus through nature-connected movement.
- Supports nervous system regulation and embodiment.
- Provides a gentle alternative to cognitive mindfulness practices.
- Can be adapted and reused in different seasons or physical states.

My notes or thoughts for implementing this session:

©2026 Integrating Nature Mental Health Counseling, PLLC. All Rights Reserved

SESSION 7

INCREASING SELF-AWARENESS

WHY IS THIS IMPORTANT?
Increasing self-awareness helps clients develop internal and external resources via nature-based activities to improve emotional functions and life satisfaction.

WHAT YOU NEED TO KNOW IN SUPPORT OF THIS SESSION

WHAT ARE THE BENEFITS OF INCREASED SELF-AWARENESS?

- Increases coping skills and the ability to manage emotions effectively.
- Enhances recognition and long-term awareness of cognitive distortions.
- Sets meaningful goals aligned with personal values.
- Proactively manages stressors and implements relaxation techniques.
- Helps make conscious decisions aligned with long-term goals and values.

HOW DOES CORE CALM INCORPORATE SELF-AWARENESS INTO NATURE-BASED THERAPY?

Through mindfulness exercises, group discussions, journaling prompts, and nature-based activities, clients can better understand their thoughts, emotions, and behaviors, enabling them to navigate challenges more effectively. Nature immersion also complements MBCT by adding a spontaneous and purposeful focus on centering and grounding the body through breathing and reflection on the present moment in nature.

WHAT IS SELF-AWARENESS?

"A reflective state of self-focused attention in which a person evaluates themself and attempts to attain correctness and consistency in beliefs and behaviors. This involves the viewing of oneself as a separate object, acknowledging limitations and the existing disparity between the ideal self and the actual self.
Objective self-awareness is often a necessary part of self-regulation."

American Psychological Association

©2026 Integrating Nature Mental Health Counseling, PLLC. All Rights Reserved

TREATMENT GOAL

After completing this session, the client will acquire enhanced self-awareness by comprehensively exploring the cognitive model, mindfulness practices, and ecotherapy applications that aim to interrupt and manage automatic thought, emotion, and behavior patterns.

GOAL OF THE SESSION

Our goal for this session is to discover increased self-awareness through an analysis of cognitive distortions.

- The client will recall how the psychological framework of MBCT helps us understand the relationship between our thoughts, emotions, and behaviors.
- The client will recall how our thoughts about a situation directly influence how we feel and respond to it, including when those thoughts are false or "distorted."
- The client will recognize how a shift in thinking can lead to more adaptive emotions and behaviors. By becoming aware of the cognitive process, we can make more intentional choices to improve our responses to challenging situations.
- The client will harness self-awareness as a tool for shifting away from automatic thoughts and move toward fact-based interpretations.

©2026 Integrating Nature Mental Health Counseling, PLLC. All Rights Reserved

SESSION 7 - ACTIVITIES

CATEGORY	Introductory	Integrative	Embodied

Activity 7:1 Deep Reflection - Honoring the Journey So Far

Purpose: Establishing presence and building awareness of internal and external experience.

Time: 20 minutes

Focus: ***Learning***

This practice invites the client to gently settle into the natural environment and use nature as a mirror for self-awareness. Through a combination of grounding and reflection, the client strengthens their capacity to notice emotional, cognitive, and somatic states without judgment. The session concludes with a guided review of previously learned therapeutic skills, deepening awareness of personal growth, and capacity for self-regulation.

Therapist Preparation:

- **Select a Supportive Natural Setting:** Choose a quiet, peaceful location with access to natural focal points—trees, rocks, or plants—that can serve as grounding anchors during mindfulness.
- **Review Previous Work Together:** Bring a notebook or paper to create a visual map or list of therapeutic skills practiced across sessions.

Client Engagement Steps:

1. **Grounding Practice in Nature:** Invite the client to find a comfortable seated position in the natural space. Ask them to gently close their eyes, breathe slowly, and allow their belly to rise on the inhale and fall on the exhale.

- Once settled, prompt the client to choose a natural object nearby—a tree, plant, or patch of ground—and direct their attention to it. Encourage them to notice visual details like texture, shape, movement, and color.
- Prompt them to expand their awareness to include sensory elements:
  - The support of the ground beneath them
  - The feeling of air on their skin
  - Surrounding sounds or scents
- Gently guide the client to turn their attention inward, noticing any tension or ease in the body, without trying to change anything. Encourage release of any tightness and remind them that no judgment is required—just presence.
- After a few moments, invite the client to open their eyes and reorient to the shared therapeutic space.

2. **Self-Reflection on Skill Development:** Using a notebook or shared writing surface, co-create a list of the six therapeutic skills explored over each of the past six sessions. The following prompt may be helpful to encourage your client: "Let's take a moment to honor the energy and work you've put into these past six sessions. What are the skills we have covered so far?"
   - Mindfulness
   - Self-Awareness
   - Ecotherapeutic Connection
   - Resilience
   - Distress Tolerance
   - Advanced Mindfulness

- Encourage the client to speak freely or write responses, connecting the following reflective questions to the grounding they just experienced.
  - "What changes have you noticed in your thoughts, reactions, relationships, or daily habits since starting this work?"
  - "How has your understanding of awareness without judgment evolved over time?"

©2026 Integrating Nature Mental Health Counseling, PLLC. All Rights Reserved

SESSION 7 - ACTIVITIES

CATEGORY	Introductory	Integrative	Embodied

Activity 7:1 Deep Reflection - Honoring the Journey So Far (Continued)

3. **Closing Integration:**
- Ask the client to name one insight, skill, or feeling of growth they want to carry forward.
- Offer a final moment of silence in the natural space, allowing time to acknowledge the environment as a witness to their progress.
- End with a grounding breath together to mark the close of the activity.

Clinical Framing & Ongoing Practice

- Reinforces the therapeutic alliance by honoring progress made together.
- Encourages somatic and cognitive integration of new skills.
- Builds a foundation of self-trust and insight by connecting body, mind, and environment.
- Prepares the client for continued work by increasing awareness of capacity and change over time.

Activity 7:2 Exploring Cognitive Distortions

Purpose: Deepening self-awareness through the MBCT model and real-time reflection.

Time: 25 minutes

Focus: ***Applying***

This activity guides the client in exploring patterns of thought that lead to emotional distress and behavioral reactivity. Using the Mindfulness-Based Cognitive Therapy (MBCT) model, the client learns to identify cognitive distortions and examine the link between thoughts, feelings, and actions. Practiced in a natural setting, this work is grounded through sensory awareness and reflective engagement with the environment.

Therapist Preparation:

- **Prepare MBCT Visual Aids:** If indoors, use a whiteboard or sketchpad. If outdoors, gather natural materials (e.g., sticks, stones, leaves) to construct a visual cycle illustrating the MBCT model **(see pg. 13 & 14 for review)** that addresses connection between thoughts → feelings → behaviors → outcomes.
- **Identify Natural Teaching Moments:** Choose a quiet location where sounds, wildlife, or changes in the environment might offer organic metaphors for perception and cognitive reaction (e.g., rustling leaves, wind through trees, animal movement).

Client Engagement Steps:

1. **Ground in the Present Moment:** Invite the client to find a comfortable seat in nature. Begin with slow, intentional breaths and gentle body awareness. Ask the client to take in their surroundings and offer a present-moment grounding prompt using the "Golden Question": "In this exact moment, what is actually happening here?"
- Encourage the client to answer with only objective, factual responses (e.g., "the breeze is moving the grass," "the sun is warming my face," "I hear birds nearby").

©2026 Integrating Nature Mental Health Counseling, PLLC. All Rights Reserved

SESSION 7 - **ACTIVITIES**

CATEGORY	Introductory	Integrative	Embodied

Activity 7:2 Exploring Cognitive Distortions (Continued)

2. **Introduce the MBCT Model Using Nature:** Use natural materials to build the MBCT cycle, in a circle. For example
   - Place an object for *Thought*
   - A second for *Feeling*
   - A third for *Behavior*
   - Use sticks or twigs to depict the cycle-shaped arrows between the three objects.

- Walk the client through a simple example together: *"Imagine you're running late. The thought might be 'I'm a failure.' That creates stress and shame. The behavior might be rushing, snapping at others, or freezing."*
- As you explain each part of the cycle, pause to let the client reflect and connect it to the placed objects and to personal experience.
- Invite them to give an example of a recent situation where they noticed this kind of automatic reaction.

3. **Identify a Cognitive Distortion:** With gentle guidance, support the client in identifying a past moment of distress where they may have experienced a cognitive distortion. This could include catastrophizing, black-and-white thinking, personalizing, or perhaps fortune-telling. Ask reframing questions such as:
   "What did you think at the time? How did that make you feel? What did you do as a result?"

- Help the client restructure the distorted thought to something more accurate or compassionate. Use the environment for metaphor: "The tree doesn't judge the wind for being too strong—it just bends and sways."

4. **Integrate the "Golden Question" Practice:** Revisit the grounding practice by asking the client to describe their current experience using only nonjudgmental observation. Invite them to reflect: "How does your experience shift when you focus on facts instead of beliefs?"

- Encourage the client to notice how thoughts can change their emotional experience in real time, even in nature. If relevant, draw attention to external triggers (a sudden sound or change in light) and ask: "What was your first thought? Was that thought accurate?"

5. **Closing Integration:** Conclude by asking the client to reflect on a key insight or moment of awareness from the activity. Invite them to name one thing they might practice differently next time they notice a distorted thought emerging.

- Offer the option to record their reflection in a journal or to create a nature-based symbol (e.g., choose a stone to represent grounded thought, a leaf to represent flexibility).
- Remind the client of the key lesson: *This isn't about stopping negative thoughts—it's about becoming aware of them and making space to respond rather than react.*

Clinical Framing for Ongoing Practice

- Strengthens cognitive-emotional awareness through embodied presence.
- Introduces and applies a core component of MBCT in a natural setting.
- Encourages practical reframing of unhelpful thoughts.
- Builds self-efficacy in managing emotional reactivity through nonjudgmental attention and grounded awareness.

My notes or thoughts for implementing this session:

©2026 Integrating Nature Mental Health Counseling, PLLC. All Rights Reserved

SESSION 7 - **ACTIVITIES**

CATEGORY	Introductory	Integrative	Embodied

Activity 7:3 Advice from the Future – A Deep Dive into Self-Awareness

Purpose: Increasing self-awareness through reflective exploration of personal history.

Time: 15 minutes

Focus: ***Becoming***

This embodied mindfulness activity invites your client to engage in deep self-awareness by revisiting a past crisis from the perspective of their present self. Set in nature, the exercise blends gentle movement, observation, and reflective writing to cultivate clarity, compassion, and growth. With the support of the natural world, your client learns to witness their personal evolution and recognize their capacity to become something new through mindful presence.

Therapist Preparation:

- **Select a Supportive Outdoor Environment:** Choose a safe, quiet area with natural landmarks where your client can move freely and find space to pause, reflect, and write undisturbed.
- **Bring Journaling Materials:** Provide a notebook and pen or pencil. Optionally, bring a cushion or mat to sit on during the writing portion of the activity.

Client Engagement Steps:

1. **Orient the Client to the Practice:** Begin by introducing the concept of self-awareness as a pathway to becoming; changing in how we see, respond, and care for ourselves over time.

   "This practice will invite you to look back at a difficult time in your life through the lens of who you are now. The aim is not to relive the experience, but to explore how you've grown and what wisdom you might offer to your past self."

2. **Begin a Reflective Walk:** Invite the client to wander slowly through the landscape. Encourage awareness of their surroundings—light, texture, air, and sound—while holding a memory of a past crisis gently in mind. As they walk:

- Encourage them to notice how the body feels in motion.
- Allow time for the memory to rise and settle without judgment.

3. **Write in Nature:** After a few minutes of walking, prompt the client to find a quiet place to sit and respond to the following reflective writing prompts:
   - *"What happened during that time, as you remember it?"*
   - *"Is there any difference in the reality of what happened versus the memory as you were holding it in your mind?*
   - *"If you could speak to your past self, what advice would you give from where you are now?"*
   - *"What strengths or insights have you gained since then?"*
   - *"What does this tell you about who you are becoming?"*

- Remind the client to stay connected to the present moment—feeling the ground beneath them, noticing the air and natural sounds—while writing.

4. **Reconnect and Share:** Invite the client to return to the shared space. Offer them the option to read aloud or summarize what they wrote, or to simply describe how the activity felt.

5. **Closing Integration:** Invite the client to choose a symbolic item from the natural space—a fallen leaf, a stone, a twig—to represent the growth or self-awareness they uncovered in the exercise, and end with a grounding breath and a reflection prompt:
   - "What part of your experience today do you want to carry forward as you continue becoming more fully yourself?"

©2026 Integrating Nature Mental Health Counseling, PLLC. All Rights Reserved

SESSION 7 - **ACTIVITIES**

CATEGORY	Introductory	Integrative	Embodied

Activity 7:3 Advice from the Future – A Deep Dive into Self-Awareness (Continued)

Clinical Framing & Ongoing Practice

- Strengthens self-awareness by linking personal history with present insight.
- Encourages mindful acceptance of one's growth, pain, and evolution.
- Supports embodiment by integrating reflection with movement and sensation.
- Reinforces the client's identity as an evolving being in relationship with nature.

My notes or thoughts for implementing this session:

©2026 Integrating Nature Mental Health Counseling, PLLC. All Rights Reserved

SESSION 8

INCREASING DISTRESS TOLERANCE

WHY IS THIS IMPORTANT?
Increasing distress tolerance equips clients with the ability to manage and navigate difficult emotions and situations more effectively while remaining present, self-aware, and fosters resilience to prevent internal and external crises.

WHAT YOU NEED TO KNOW IN SUPPORT OF THIS SESSION

WHAT ARE THE BENEFITS OF INCREASING DISTRESS TOLERANCE?

- Improves resilience in navigating stressful situations.
- Enhances the ability to manage stress and discomfort effectively.
- Reduces the likelihood of engaging in impulsive or harmful behaviors during distressing circumstances.
- Heightens emotional regulation and stability.
- Increases capacity for problem-solving and decision-making under pressure.
- Strengthens overall mental well-being and adaptability to life's challenges.

HOW DOES CORE CALM INCORPORATE THE USE OF INCREASED DISTRESS TOLERANCE INTO NATURE-BASED THERAPY?

Nature-based activities challenge and engage g clients as they are guided to remain present with discomfort using the environment as a supportive space to build resilience and regulation.

As clients navigate organic but stressful circumstances (stubbed toe, trouble building a fire, etc.) emotionally, kinesthetically, and cognitively they are encouraged to think, act, and feel to find a solution. Upon completing the exercise, reflective processing is used to deepen self-awareness and personal growth.

WHAT IS INCREASED DISTRESS TOLERANCE?

Increasing distress tolerance means managing emotional discomfort without being overwhelmed. This practice fosters resilience by allowing for progressively greater use of coping skills to navigate adversity without resorting to harmful behaviors. Strengthening distress tolerance enhances resilience under challenging circumstances.

Distress tolerance skills, derived from Dialectical Behavior Therapy (DBT), help clients manage emotional distress without worsening the situation, especially during crises. Techniques include accepting reality, breathwork, self-soothing techniques, radical acceptance, and logical distraction

These skills can be learned through various methods and are invaluable for promoting resilience and effective coping mechanisms in challenging situations.

©2026 Integrating Nature Mental Health Counseling, PLLC. All Rights Reserved

TREATMENT GOAL

After completing this session, the client will be able to harness advanced coping skills in resilience to navigate emotionally charged situations.

GOAL OF THE SESSION

Our goal for this session is to increase distress tolerance.

- The client will develop and strengthen distress tolerance skills by mindfully engaging with challenging or uncomfortable experiences in nature, learning to observe internal responses (e.g., anxiety, frustration, fear) without avoidance or reactivity, and practicing emotional regulation in the face of stress.

©2026 Integrating Nature Mental Health Counseling, PLLC. All Rights Reserved

SESSION 8 - ACTIVITIES

CATEGORY	Introductory	Integrative	Embodied

Activity 8:1 Trusting the Unknown – A Blindfold Walk

Purpose: Establishing presence and building awareness of internal and external experience.

Time: 15 minutes

Focus: ***Learning***

This introductory activity uses movement through a natural space without sight to help the client explore how uncertainty affects their thoughts, emotions, and body. It promotes awareness of the body's stress response, supports practice in emotional regulation, and lays a foundation for learning how to manage discomfort while remaining present.

Therapist Preparation:

- **Select a Safe, Navigable Trail:** Choose a short, obstacle-free section of a wooded trail or open area with gentle terrain and clear ground. Walk the path first and remove hazards to ensure safety.
- **Prepare a Blindfold or Adaptation Options:** Bring a soft blindfold or scarf. Offer alternatives (e.g., keeping eyes closed or using a wide-brimmed hat) for clients who may feel anxious or triggered. Reinforce that this is a "challenge by choice" activity.

Client Engagement Steps:

1. **Introduce the Concept:** Invite your client to consider how it feels to move through uncertainty without control. Explain that the activity is designed to help them notice how their body and mind respond to unfamiliar or stressful situations.

   "In this activity, we'll use nature and movement to learn about how you respond to uncertainty. You'll walk slowly through a natural space without seeing where you're going. I'll be here the entire time as your guide."

2. **Begin the Practice:**
- Help your client choose their preferred visual limitation (blindfold, eyes closed, hat).
- Invite them to stand upright, relax their bodies, and take a few deep breaths as they orient themselves to the space using all other senses except sight.
- Offer a rope or light physical guidance with consent, and begin to walk slowly through the forest. **Tip**: It is helpful to explain how you will be guiding your client prior to limiting their sight. This will include asking permission to touch them.
- Remain quiet but attuned, gently naming natural sounds or textures when helpful (e.g., "soft pine needles," "rustling breeze") and instructing them with guidance if they need to step over, go around/under, or be otherwise cautious about potential hazards. **Tip**: Be aware of issues such as poison ivy or thorned foliage.

3. **Encourage Somatic Awareness:** As your client walks, it may be helpful to stop occasionally for a grounding breath. Don't forget to encourage deep sensory awareness of their environment, such as:
- The way the ground feels beneath their feet
- The sounds around them
- Changes in body temperature or muscle tension
- Emotional shifts, such as hesitation, curiosity, or calm

4. **Complete the Walk and Re-Orient:** When the walk is finished, invite your client to stop, remove the blindfold, and take a few grounding breaths. Give them space to visually take in the natural setting before transitioning into reflection.

©2026 Integrating Nature Mental Health Counseling, PLLC. All Rights Reserved

SESSION 8 - **ACTIVITIES**

CATEGORY	Introductory	Integrative	Embodied

Activity 8:1 Trusting the Unknown – A Blindfold Walk (Continued)

5. **Reflect and Integrate:** Invite your client to journal and discuss their response to questions such as:

- What was the most noticeable physical sensation?
- What emotions arose while walking without sight?
- How did it feel to surrender control and rely on other senses?
- What connections can be made between this experience and moments of stress in daily life?

6. **Closing Integration:** Invite the client to choose one small natural object from the area—such as a stone, leaf, or pinecone—that represents a personal insight gained from the activity. Use this object as a symbolic reminder of their ability to navigate discomfort with presence and awareness.

- Offer a closing breath and affirmation: "Today you learned that you can be present and steady, even in the unknown."

Clinical Framing & Ongoing Practice

- Supports early awareness of how stress and uncertainty are experienced in the body.
- Builds tolerance for discomfort without emotional reactivity.
- Enhances interoceptive awareness and somatic grounding.
- Encourages the development of safety, trust, and therapeutic rapport in natural settings.
- Offers a meaningful, embodied introduction to distress tolerance skills.

My notes or thoughts for implementing this session:

©2026 Integrating Nature Mental Health Counseling, PLLC. All Rights Reserved

SESSION 8 - **ACTIVITIES**

CATEGORY	Introductory	Integrative	Embodied

Activity 8:2 Walking the Line – Learning Balance in Body and Mind

Purpose: Using somatic awareness to increase emotional regulation.

Time: 20 minutes

Focus: ***Applying***

This integrative activity uses physical balance in a natural setting as a metaphor for emotional balance. It supports the development of distress tolerance by integrating mindfulness, body awareness, and cognitive-emotional observation in real-time. Through a progression of prompts, the client explores the ways emotional states can influence physical grounding and equilibrium.

Therapist Preparation:

- **Choose an Appropriate Log:** Identify a stable, straight, fallen log or similar natural feature in advance. Ensure it is low to the ground and clear of sharp branches or obstacles. (A line dragged in the dirt or with chalk is a good alternative).
- **Introduce the Metaphor:** Explain that the log symbolizes emotional balance. This activity connects physical balance with the mental and emotional skills and focus needed for distress tolerance.

Client Engagement Steps:

1. **Orient to the Space:** Invite your client to walk with you to select a log for balancing on. **Tip**: To minimize risk, be sure the log is not rotted or slippery, is big and sturdy enough to hold the weight of the client, is lying flush with the ground, and is nowhere near a slope. **As an alternative, you can use a simple line drawn with spray chalk or by dragging your foot in the dirt.

2. **Initial Balance Practice:** Before you invite your client to step onto the log, frame the activity: "Today, we'll explore how physical balance can mirror emotional balance. As you stand/walk on this log, notice how your body responds—and how that connects to your thoughts and emotions."

- Have your client step up on the log (or straddle/sit if balance is limited). Guide them to find a steady standing position with knees slightly bent, core engaged, and gaze forward. Encourage quiet attention to breath, feet, and body alignment. Allow them to practice balancing for a few minutes, noting sensations and any internal shifts.

3. **Introduce Mental Challenge:** Once steady on the log, ask your client to briefly recall a *difficult* or emotionally charged memory—something mildly distressing but not overwhelming. Invite them to observe what changes in their balance, breath, or thoughts as the memory arises. Reflect together on how emotional triggers impact their focus and their body's ability to maintain balance.

4. **Joyful Reframe Practice:** Now, ask your client to recall a *joyful* or peaceful memory. Again, notice how that thought affects their posture, muscle tension, and overall balance. Encourage open curiosity about how positive emotional states influence focus and physical stability.

5. **Repeat with Eyes Closed (Optional Challenge):** For clients who are physically capable, suggest closing their eyes while on the log for a few seconds. Remind them to listen to their body and open eyes or step off if they feel unsafe. Reflect on how the absence of visual input increases reliance on internal cues, paralleling how self-awareness can help us navigate uncertainty.

6. **Step Off and Debrief:** Invite the client to step down and sit on a nearby log or the ground. Ask reflective questions:
   - "What did you notice about your body and thoughts while balancing?"
   - "How did your internal experience change with different memories?"

©2026 Integrating Nature Mental Health Counseling, PLLC. All Rights Reserved

SESSION 8 - ACTIVITIES

CATEGORY	Introductory	Integrative	Embodied

Activity 8:2 Walking the Line – Learning Balance in Body and Mind (Continued)

- "What helps you regain balance—physically and emotionally?"
- Encourage them to make connections between this physical experience and moments of emotional distress in daily life.

7. **Closing Integration:** Offer a short grounding practice, such as placing both feet on the earth and taking three slow breaths together. Reaffirm that emotional balance, like physical balance, can be learned and strengthened over time through awareness and practice.

Clinical Framing for Ongoing Practice

- Reinforces the mind-body connection as a tool for emotional self-regulation.
- Teaches that distress tolerance requires intentional shifts in attention and posture.
- Promotes experiential learning through metaphor and direct somatic engagement.
- Encourages building tolerance for uncertainty by safely practicing physical imbalance.

Activity 8:3 Rock Cairn Reflection

Purpose: To strengthen awareness of distress tolerance through embodied balance and symbolic creation.

Time: 25 minutes

Focus: ***Becoming***

This embodied practice invites your client to integrate distress tolerance skills through creative engagement with natural materials. By mindfully collecting and balancing stones into a cairn, the client externalizes emotional regulation and resilience-building. The activity emphasizes awareness of bodily sensations, grounding through movement, and symbolic reflection, encouraging presence, patience, and trust in the self.

Therapist Preparation:

- **Scout and Prepare the Area:** Locate a trail or wooded clearing with scattered rocks and grounded, rooted trees for sitting. Walk the area beforehand to ensure safe footing and available natural materials.
- **Orient the Intention:** Remind your client that this is a practice in embodied awareness—engaging movement, stillness, and the elements to connect distress tolerance to the wisdom of the body and land.

Client Engagement Steps:

1. **Grounding Through Movement:** Begin by inviting your client to transition from the previous activity by standing tall, stretching, and taking a few centering breaths. Acknowledge that balancing on the log may have activated physical tension or alertness in the body. Encourage them to gently roll their willers, shake out their limbs, or bend side to side to help decompress areas of tightness. As they begin to walk, remind them to allow each step to release tension and recalibrate—an embodied return to steadiness.

©2026 Integrating Nature Mental Health Counseling, PLLC. All Rights Reserved

SESSION 8 - **ACTIVITIES**

CATEGORY	Introductory	Integrative	Embodied

Activity 8:3 Rock Cairn Reflection (Continued)

2. **Gathering With Intention:** Ask the client to walk through the natural space around them, collecting a rock for each internal strength or coping skill they've practiced (e.g., self-regulation, radical acceptance, grounding, reframing). Rocks should be no bigger than the palm of a hand and somewhat shapely, not flat or planar.

3. **Cairn Building as Somatic Dialogue:** Once they've collected 4–5 rocks, invite your client to stack the rocks slowly, using breath, presence, and patience. Encourage them to notice texture, weight, balance, and tension in their hands and arms. Each rock becomes a physical reflection of their growing ability to stay steady through internal challenge. If the stack wobbles or falls, they can begin again—this too is part of the practice.

4. **Closing and Integration:** Once the cairn is complete, invite your client to sit in stillness beside it, and consider how these rocks, each representing a skill, are now the embodiment of an internal balance. Guide a few grounding breaths and prompt reflection:
   - *"Which part of your body felt most activated during this process?"*
   - *"What did your body teach you today?"*
   - *"In what way are you becoming more capable of tolerating discomfort?"*

- Invite your client to name their skills aloud, and either leave their cairn as an offering or take a photo or rock with them as a symbol of this moment. Walk back together slowly, remaining attuned to how the body feels in movement.

Clinical Framing & Ongoing Practice

- Links symbolic representation of distress tolerance skills with physical, embodied action.
- Helps client somatically rehearse emotional balance and recovery through breath, rhythm, and grounded focus.
- Engages the body as a site of wisdom, endurance, and communication.
- Reinforces the core theme of *becoming* through sensory and somatic integration of inner growth.

My notes or thoughts for implementing this session:

©2026 Integrating Nature Mental Health Counseling, PLLC. All Rights Reserved

NOTES & TAKEAWAYS

My Thoughts & Reflections:

©2026 Integrating Nature Mental Health Counseling, PLLC. All Rights Reserved

SESSION 9

ACTIVE ENGAGEMENT

WHY IS THIS IMPORTANT?

Your client's intentional participation in therapeutic activities will strengthen active engagement as a coping mechanism, which supports their ability to manage emotional challenges, regulate responses, and remain present and responsive in moments of discomfort.

WHAT YOU NEED TO KNOW IN SUPPORT OF THIS SESSION

WHAT ARE THE BENEFITS OF ACTIVE ENGAGEMENT?

- Enhances learning and retention of information.
- Increases motivation and persistence in tasks.
- Improves critical thinking skills and abilities.
- Promotes positive emotions and stress reduction.

HOW DOES CORE CALM INCORPORATE ACTIVE ENGAGEMENT INTO NATURE-BASED THERAPY?

Core Calm promotes active engagement by encouraging committed action and adaptable problem-solving aligned with ACT principles while fostering mindfulness. It enhances clients' engagement, social interaction, and skill development, offering practical skills for real-life application.

WHAT IS ACTIVE ENGAGEMENT?

Active engagement refers to the state of being fully involved and immersed in a particular activity or process. It implies active participation, attentiveness, and involvement with the task.

Depending on the nature of the activity or situation, active engagement may involve physical, mental, or emotional participation. It often signifies a higher level of involvement and commitment than passive or superficial engagement.

©2026 Integrating Nature Mental Health Counseling, PLLC. All Rights Reserved

TREATMENT GOAL

After completing this session, the client will be able to foster a strong and collaborative therapeutic relationship with nature, empowering the client to actively participate in their care and achieve positive outcomes. This involves the client feeling safe, supported, and comfortable, leading to greater adherence to treatment, increased satisfaction, and ultimately, better therapeutic results.

GOAL OF THE SESSION

Our goal for this session is to encourage committed action and adaptable problem-solving.

- The client will remember that they have developed a toolkit of strategies to draw upon, and that while this is a hands-on learning experience, it is also a challenge by choice.
- The client will view this as an opportunity put knowledge into practice and deepen it, which is how we engage in the process of healing.

©2026 Integrating Nature Mental Health Counseling, PLLC. All Rights Reserved

SESSION 9 - **ACTIVITIES**

CATEGORY	Introductory	Integrative and Embodied

Activity 9:1 Practicing Active Engagement with the Present Moment

Purpose: To ground the nervous system through sensory awareness and intentional connection with the natural world.

Time: 15 minutes

Focus: ***Learning***

This practice introduces your client to the foundational skill of active engagement through grounding in nature. By using breath, imagery, and sensory awareness, your client is gently guided to shift attention away from internal chatter and into the immediate environment. This promotes regulation, connection, and the capacity to be fully present—essential building blocks for deeper nature-based therapeutic work.

Therapist Preparation:

- **Site Selection:** Select a calming natural area where your client can sit or lie down comfortably. A forest floor, grassy clearing, or soft ground near water is ideal. Choose a space with minimal distraction, but enough sensory richness to engage visual, tactile, and auditory awareness.
- **Prepare the Client for Stillness:** Introduce the idea that this exercise is not about achieving a particular state, but about learning to *notice* what is already happening in the body and environment. Emphasize permission to move or adjust posture if discomfort arises.

Client Engagement Steps:

1. **Set Intentions:** Begin by asking the client to center their focus on their body instead of their thoughts. Offer this frame: "Let's begin today by practicing how we shift our focus from what's happening in our heads to what's happening around and within us, right now. We'll use the natural environment to help us ground and get present."

2. **Grounding & Positioning:** Invite your client to find a comfortable position—sitting with both feet planted firmly on the ground, or lying down if the space allows. Suggest they close their eyes or let their gaze soften on the forest, sky, or nearby tree canopy—whichever feels more natural.

3. **Sensory Activation:** Gently guide their attention to the body and the environment. Prompts may include:
   - "Let your breath slow down just a bit, and feel the weight of your body where it meets the earth."
   - "Feel the pressure where your back, seat, or feet connect with the ground."
   - "Notice how your breath moves through your body—what changes with each inhale and exhale?"
   - "What do you hear around you? Take in the textures of sound without labeling them."
   - "Can you sense a breeze? Sunlight? Shade? What do you feel on your skin?"

- Introduce a brief nature-based visualization:
  - "Imagine yourself as a tree. Strong roots growing from your feet into the ground beneath you. These roots hold you here—steady, supported, connected."
- Allow 30–60 seconds of quiet stillness for your client to explore that imagery and embodied sensation.

4. **Return to the Present:** Guide the client gently back to a more alert state by inviting them to slowly begin to wiggle their fingers and toes to feel the return of movement. When they are ready, they may open their eyes or lift their gaze. Offer the prompt: "Notice how it feels to come back into this space. Let's take a moment just to look around—what do you see, hear, or feel now that you didn't notice before?"

©2026 Integrating Nature Mental Health Counseling, PLLC. All Rights Reserved

SESSION 9 - ACTIVITIES

CATEGORY | Introductory | Integrative and Embodied

Activity 9:1 Practicing Active Engagement with the Present Moment (Continued)

5. **Closing Integration:** Offer a brief explanation of the practice: "This kind of grounding helps bring your attention to what's real and present, which is especially helpful when thoughts or stress start to pull you away. The natural world offers constant invitations to come back to the here and now—we just practice accepting them."

- Encourage your client to try similar grounding when alone outdoors or when feeling overwhelmed, using breath and observation to return to the body and moment.

Clinical Framing & Ongoing Practice

- Introduces basic active engagement through embodied presence and sensory immersion.
- Supports nervous system regulation by anchoring attention in the body and environment.
- Builds foundational mindfulness skills necessary for more advanced therapeutic work.
- Encourages relational connection with nature as a co-regulating force.
- Can be adapted for use at the beginning or end of sessions to support emotional transition.

Activity 9:2 Stealth and Stillness: Active Engagement in the Wild

Purpose: To apply active engagement skills by integrating sensory awareness, mindful regulation, and embodied presence through a playful nature-based challenge.

Time: 45 minutes

Focus: ***Applying & Becoming***

This activity invites your client to deepen their connection to internal sensations and the natural environment by practicing mindful stalking and regulation of the body's survival responses. Through sensory immersion and active participation, your client will engage their fight, flight, freeze, or fawn responses in a safe setting while learning to notice and modulate physical and emotional reactions.

Therapist Preparation:

- **Site Selection:** Choose a natural outdoor area with enough space to create a roughly 30 ft by 12 ft rectangular playing field with lines made of sticks, branches, or other natural materials. The ground should be safe for slow, deliberate movement (clear of sharp rocks or hazards).
- **Prepare the Client:** Explain the purpose of the exercise as an opportunity to notice and regulate bodily sensations connected to perceived threat responses while practicing quiet movement and control of breath and heart rate. *Emphasize there is no real danger, only mindful engagement that elicits natural instincts.*

Client Engagement Steps:

1. **Set Intentions:** Invite your client to center their focus on their body and breath before beginning. You might say: "Let's set an intention to explore how your body and mind respond when you move quietly and attentively in nature. Notice what sensations come up as you practice staying calm and aware."

2. **Prepare the Playing Field (7 minutes):** Guide your client in creating the boundaries of the playing field using natural materials, about 30 feet long and 12 feet wide. This defines the space where the stalking game will take place.

©2026 Integrating Nature Mental Health Counseling, PLLC. All Rights Reserved

SESSION 9 - **ACTIVITIES**

CATEGORY	Introductory	Integrative and Embodied

Activity 9:2 Stealth and Stillness: Active Engagement in the Wild (Continued)

3. **Practice Quiet Movement (10 minutes):** Teach and practice "fox walking" or mindful walking techniques with your client. Encourage controlled, mindful steps and breath awareness to help regulate heart rate and body tension. **Tip**: If the client is willing, barefoot practice is best – don't be afraid to try this for yourself first and be a role model!

- Offer the following instruction:
  - *"Focus on your breath and take slow, gentle steps, touching your pinky toe first and then rolling slowly over the pad of your foot, and finally lowering your heel. At this point, all of your weight should be placed on one foot/leg while the other is free to move forward. Notice how your body feels as you move quietly through the space."*

4. **Explain the Game (3 minutes):**

a) Position yourself seated and blindfolded at one end of the playing field.

b) Stick a matchstick into the ground in front of you (about 1 foot away).

c) Explain that the client's goal is to quietly approach and steal the matchstick without being detected.

d) If you sense movement, you will point, and the client must return to the start and try again.

5. **Engage in the Stalk (15 minutes):** Allow your client to attempt the stalk, coaching them to notice bodily sensations like heart rate, breath, and muscle tension.

- Remind them: *"Remember, this is a safe space. Your body might feel*
- *excited or nervous, and that's okay. Use your breath to stay calm, regulate heart rate and stay connected to your actions in the present moment."*

WHERE YOUR BODY 'FEELS' EMOTIONS

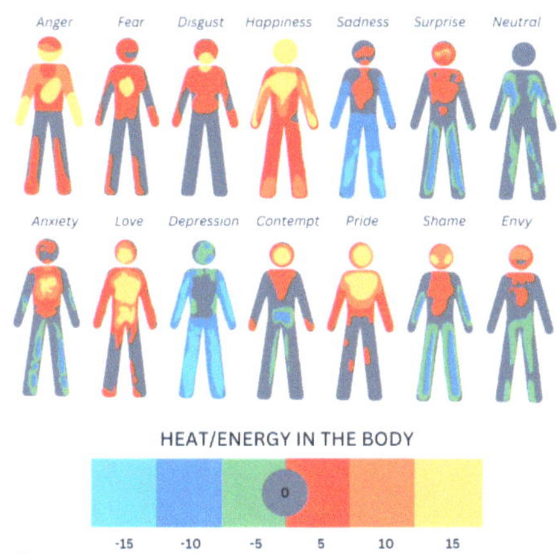

6. **Optional Role Reversal:** Invite your client to try being the blindfolded sentinel while you attempt to steal a match. This role switch can deepen sensory awareness and trust.

7. **Debrief and Reflect (10 minutes):** After the activity, guide your client in reflecting on their experience.
   - What physical sensations did they notice?
   - What coping skills did they have to draw on to regulate their body's threat response?
   - How did they manage feelings of anticipation or fear?
   - Which strategies helped maintain calm and focus?
   - What happened to their breath and heartbeat after several turns?

Clinical Framing & Ongoing Practice

- Integrates active engagement through embodied awareness and sensory immersion.
- Supports real-time regulation of the nervous system by applying breath and movement strategies.
- Encourages experiential learning about survival instincts and mindful presence in nature.
- Builds resilience and distress tolerance by exposing the client to controlled, manageable challenges.
- Can be adapted for individual or small group therapy and varied by terrain, footwear, or role-switching.

©2026 Integrating Nature Mental Health Counseling, PLLC. All Rights Reserved

SESSION 10

MAINTAINING FOCUS

WHY IS THIS IMPORTANT?
The ability to focus and maintain concentration is a fundamental aspect of cognitive functioning that plays a crucial role in various domains of life, from academic and professional success to personal well-being. Understanding the mechanisms underlying attentional control empowers your clients to develop strategies that optimize their focus and help them to achieve their goals more effectively.

WHAT YOU NEED TO KNOW IN SUPPORT OF THIS SESSION

WHAT ARE THE BENEFITS OF HAVING THE ABILITY TO MAINTAIN FOCUS?

- Enhances productivity and efficiency in completing tasks.
- Improves performance across various areas of life, such as work, academics, and personal goals.
- Betters time management and prioritization of tasks.
- Reduces stress and overwhelm through organized focus and control.

HOW DOES CORE CALM INCORPORATE MAINTAINING FOCUS INTO NATURE-BASED THERAPY?

Core Calm utilizes practices and challenges immersed in nature to anchor attention to the present despite a wandering mind, helping clients strengthen concentration and presence through sustained engagement with the environment.

WHAT IS THE ABILITY TO MAINTAIN FOCUS?

The ability to maintain focus refers to the capacity to concentrate on a task or activity for an extended period without being easily distracted by intrusive thoughts or dysregulated emotions.

In psychology, this ability is often understood through the lens of attentional control, which involves the capacity to attend to relevant stimuli while inhibiting distractions selectively. Factors, such as individual differences in temperament, environmental stimuli, and cognitive processes, influence one's ability to sustain focus. Techniques, such as mindfulness meditation, cognitive-behavioral strategies, and environmental modifications, have been explored to enhance focus and concentration.

©2026 Integrating Nature Mental Health Counseling, PLLC. All Rights Reserved

TREATMENT GOAL

After completing this session, the client will be able to demonstrate strengthened ability to sustain present-moment attention by using natural elements as grounding anchors, thereby improving concentration, emotional regulation, and resilience.

GOAL OF THE SESSION

Our goal for this session is to enhance our client's ability to cultivate sustained attention and presence by practicing focus within a natural setting.

- The client will be able to identify personal strengths and resilience. despite moments of doubt.
- The client will use 'The Highlights Reel' as an effective strategy to focus more intently on what they are doing right, rather than what they are doing wrong.
- The client will learn that resilience is all about bouncing back after tough times. By focusing on our wins more than our mistakes they celebrate accomplishments, experience growth, and find the strength to tackle the challenges ahead.

©2026 Integrating Nature Mental Health Counseling, PLLC. All Rights Reserved

SESSION 10 - ACTIVITIES

CATEGORY	Introductory	Integrative	Embodied

Activity 10:1 The Nature Sort – Building Focus Through Sensory Engagement

Purpose: Cultivating control of attention and focus on the present moment through task-based movement and intentional sensory processing.

Time: 15 minutes

Focus: ***Learning***

This structured, hands-on activity invites your client to strengthen focused attention using touch, texture, and visual differentiation. By collecting and sorting natural objects based on physical qualities, the client practices regulating attention and tracking task-based focus in real-time. The process also encourages present-moment awareness, sensory regulation, and quiet internal reflection—essential building blocks for maintaining focus in both therapeutic and everyday environments.

Therapist Preparation:

- **Select a Varied Landscape:** Choose a setting with ample natural materials that vary in size, texture, shape, and color. Ideal spaces include a forest floor, meadow, or lakeside area where clients can safely move and gather materials.
- **Define the Workspace:** Bring a cloth, tarp, or flat natural surface (like a large rock or log) to use as a sorting area. If needed, outline 2–3 small zones using rope, stones, or sticks to mark where sorted items will be placed.
- **Set Boundaries:** Identify a small, walkable perimeter (approx. 10–20 feet) where the client can safely collect materials without distraction.

Client Engagement Steps:

1. **Set Intentions:** Begin by introducing the purpose of the activity in simple, focused terms. Let your client know that the goal is not to complete a perfect task, but to notice how attention works in real time—how it holds, drifts, and returns. *"This activity is about practicing how to focus—using your hands and senses to stay with a task, even when distractions or inner thoughts show up. You'll use what's around you to notice how your attention moves and how you can bring it back."*

2. **Collect Natural Items:** Instruct your client to explore this space while collecting 10–12 natural items from the surrounding area. Items should vary in characteristics such as shape, weight, texture, and temperature.

- Emphasize safety (e.g., be aware of where they are walking, no sharp, poisonous, or extremely heavy items).
- Encourage them to move slowly and remain focused on what their hands *feel*, rather than naming or analyzing objects.
- Keep verbal guidance minimal to support internal focus.

3. **Sort by Qualities:** Invite your client to sit at the prepared sorting space and begin grouping the objects into 2–3 self-selected categories based on tactile or visual qualities.

- Avoid offering specific sorting instructions unless requested.
- Observe how the client engages—whether they move quickly, pause often, become distracted, or remain focused.
- Allow them to adjust categories mid-process if needed.

4. **Internal Check-In:** Once sorting is complete, invite the client to sit quietly and observe their sorted objects.

- Encourage internal noticing over verbal discussion. Remember to offer a few focused processing questions, such as:
  - *"What helped you stay focused during this activity?"*
  - *"Where did your attention go when it wandered?"*
  - *"What do you notice in your body now that you've completed the task?"*

©2026 Integrating Nature Mental Health Counseling, PLLC. All Rights Reserved

SESSION 10 - ACTIVITIES

CATEGORY	Introductory	Integrative	Embodied

Activity 10:1 The Nature Sort – Building Focus Through Sensory Engagement (Continued)

5. **Close the Practice**: Invite your client to select one object from their collection to carry with them or place in a shared spot. Let this be a reminder of their ability to refocus and complete a task even when attention drifts.

- Gently transition out of the activity with a deep breath and brief reflection on the experience.

Clinical Framing & Ongoing Practice

- Builds task-based focus and sustained attention in a quiet, nonverbal context.
- Encourages somatic and sensory engagement to reduce cognitive overload.
- Provides insight into personal attention patterns and regulation strategies.
- Useful as an introductory mindfulness exercise or pre-session grounding tool.
- Can be repeated with symbolic sorting themes in later sessions (e.g., values, emotions, priorities).

Activity 10:2 The Highlights Trail – Maintaining Focus on Strength Through Reflective Memory

Purpose: Strengthening focus on personal resilience by integrating reflective memory, symbolic movement, and values-based accomplishment.

Time: 30 minutes

Focus: ***Applying***

This activity supports your client in actively applying the skill of maintaining focus on what has gone well, rather than defaulting to what has gone wrong. By walking a symbolic trail while recalling moments of strength and success, your client builds cognitive flexibility, emotional regulation, and long-term resilience. This integrative practice encourages the client to view their internal "highlights reel" as a living source of self-efficacy that can be drawn upon when focus falters.

Therapist Preparation:

- **Choose the Setting:** Select a quiet walking path in nature—ideally a short loop or linear trail with room for pausing and reflective movement. Ensure the terrain is flat and comfortable for slow pacing. Choose a location where natural elements like trees, rocks, or turns in the trail can symbolically mark transitions between life stages or personal milestones.
- **Bring Minimal Materials:** Have a small notebook and pen or pencil available for your client. Optionally, prepare flat stones, leaves, or small tokens that the client can carry or place as symbolic markers during the walk.

Client Engagement Steps:

1. **Set Intentions:** Begin by inviting your client to enter a reflective mindset as you prepare to walk together. Explain that the purpose of the activity is to practice maintaining focus on personal strengths and resilience, not just during moments of success, but as a conscious habit that supports well-being over time. Introduce the metaphor of the "highlights reel" used in professional sports:

   "This activity is about staying focused on what's working—what you've already done well. Just like athletes review their best performances to stay mentally strong, you'll walk a path today that invites you to recall moments of pride, perseverance, and growth."

©2026 Integrating Nature Mental Health Counseling, PLLC. All Rights Reserved

SESSION 10 - ACTIVITIES

CATEGORY	Introductory	Integrative	Embodied

Activity 10:2 The Highlights Trail – Maintaining Focus on Strength Through Reflective Memory (Cont'd)

- Briefly explain that you'll walk together and pause at intervals to reflect on different time periods of life. At each pause, the client will recall an accomplishment and note a word or phrase in their notebook.

2. **The Reflective Walk:** Begin walking together at a slow, steady pace. After a few minutes, stop at a chosen point (tree, stone, bend in the trail) and invite the first memory.

- **First Stop – Early Childhood:** Ask your client to recall a moment from early childhood that brought pride, joy, or a feeling of accomplishment.
  - Allow quiet space for reflection.
  - Prompt them to write a short story capturing that memory.
  - Encourage embodiment: *"Notice where you feel that memory in your body as you recall it."*

- **Second Stop – Teenage Years:** Resume walking and stop again at a new symbolic marker. Invite your client to recall a success from adolescence. This could be academic, social, creative, or physical.
  - Again, pause. Have them write a short story about this experience and optionally place a token in the space.
  - If using natural markers, the client may place a stone or leaf along the trail to represent this moment.

- **Third Stop – Adulthood:** Proceed to the third location. Prompt the client to reflect on a time in adulthood when they overcame a challenge, persisted through difficulty, or achieved something they once thought was out of reach.
  - Encourage attention to inner resources: *"What strength did you draw on? What supported you?"*
  - Have them write about this experience and optionally place a token in the space.

- **Fourth Stop – Recent Accomplishment:** Stop at a final location in view of the trail's end or a quiet sitting space. Invite your client to reflect on something they are proud of from the last nine sessions of work together, whether therapeutic, personal, or simply showing up with consistency.
  - Ask them to choose one word or phrase that captures this moment and write it down.
  - Allow a longer pause here for integration before walking back together.

3. **Close the Practice:** Invite your client to sit and discuss with you the experiences or memories they've recorded. Reflect with them on the meaning of these moments and how they can serve as focus points when doubt, overwhelm, or distraction arise. Optional prompts could include: "If you were creating a 'highlights reel' to keep your mind centered in hard times, what moment from today would lead it?"

- Encourage them to revisit this "trail" internally whenever they lose sight of their progress.

Clinical Framing for Ongoing Practice

- Helps anchor the client's focus on progress, effort, and strength.
- Encourages self-recognition through memory-based resilience recall.
- Reinforces psychological flexibility by shifting attention toward effective past strategies.
- Combines symbolic movement with values-based reflection.
- Can be repeated with seasonal or developmental themes or used as a closing ritual at the end of treatment.

©2026 Integrating Nature Mental Health Counseling, PLLC. All Rights Reserved

SESSION 10 - ACTIVITIES

CATEGORY	Introductory	Integrative	Embodied

Activity 10:3 Releasing to Refocus – A Shift Toward What Matters

Purpose: Applying focused attention through symbolic release and intentional redirection of energy.

Time: 15 minutes

Focus: ***Applying***

This activity supports your client in practicing embodied focus by identifying internal distractions, letting go of what impedes progress, and making space to re-align with purposeful attention. Through movement, symbolic writing, and a nature-based release ritual, the client strengthens their ability to shift focus intentionally, from what weighs them down to what supports becoming. This practice deepens the connection between attention, emotional release, and future readiness.

Therapist Preparation:

- **Select a Private, Contained Setting:** Choose a quiet natural area that allows for reflection and safe symbolic release—ideally with access to a fire pit, stream, or alternative release site (e.g., buried in earth, scattered in wind, composted). Ensure emotional privacy and environmental safety.
- **Gather Materials:** Bring a notebook or several small slips of paper (approx. 3x3 or 4x6 inches), pencils or pens, and fire-safe materials (if using fire). Optional: flat stone, stump, or bench for writing support.
- **Prepare Client for Emotional Depth:** Let your client know that this practice will involve identifying and physically releasing internal obstacles that interfere with their ability to stay focused on what matters. Emphasize emotional safety and full choice throughout.

Client Engagement Steps:

1. **Set Intentions:** Introduce the activity by framing focus as something that requires *not just effort, but space*. Letting go of distractions, past attachments, or limiting beliefs allows the mind and body to focus more clearly on meaningful direction. *"This practice is about making space for what matters by letting go of what no longer serves you. When we hold on to emotional clutter or unhelpful thoughts, it's harder to focus on where we're going. Today, you'll name what you're ready to release—and you'll use a physical ritual to help your body feel that shift."*

2. **Identify Distractions:** Invite your client to sit quietly with their notebook or paper. Provide four blank slips or pages. Instruct them to reflect on their recent challenges and write down <u>four internal obstacles</u> that make it hard to stay focused or move forward. These might include emotions, habits, thoughts, or beliefs.

- Encourage honesty and brevity—one idea per slip.
- Let this be a silent process. Offer emotional containment through calm presence.
- If needed, gently prompt with: *"What thought or feeling pulls your attention away from what's important?"*

3. **Embodied Release Ritual:** Guide your client to a symbolic release space (fire pit, stream, or tree base). Let them know they will release each slip of paper one at a time, offering it as a gesture of release and redirection.

- Invite them to pause with each slip before releasing it.
- If using fire: Have the client drop each slip into the flames one by one, with a short pause between.
- If not using fire: Use an alternate symbolic act (burying, tearing, casting into water or wind). Offer the frame: "*This is your physical way of telling your body and mind: I'm done carrying this.*"

4. **Integrate the Shift:** Once all four slips are released, invite your client to walk back to a neutral grounding space. Ask them to identify **one thing they now feel more able to focus on**—a goal, a value, or a way of being. Let them write it on a fresh piece of paper or speak it aloud if they choose.
"This is your re-focus point. It's what has space now that you've let go."

©2026 Integrating Nature Mental Health Counseling, PLLC. All Rights Reserved

SESSION 10 - **ACTIVITIES**

CATEGORY	Introductory	Integrative	Embodied

Activity 10:3 Releasing to Refocus – A Shift Toward What Matters (Continued)

5. **Close the Practice:**

- Offer a final reflection, such as: *"Letting go is part of becoming. When we release what's heavy or unhelpful, we're choosing to give more of our energy to what matters. You've just practiced that—not only in thought, but in movement and action."*
- *Invite the client to revisit this practice anytime they feel their focus clouded by emotional residue or internal noise.*

Clinical Framing & Ongoing Practice

- Supports focus maintenance by actively clearing emotional or cognitive distractions.
- Strengthens embodied agency through symbolic action and sensory integration.
- Encourages interoceptive awareness and alignment with personal values.
- Teaches the client to recognize release as a skill—one that makes space for clarity and direction.
- Can be repeated as a ritual during seasonal transitions, treatment milestones, or before goal setting.

My notes or thoughts for implementing this session:

©2026 Integrating Nature Mental Health Counseling, PLLC. All Rights Reserved

NOTES & TAKEAWAYS

My Thoughts & Reflections:

©2026 Integrating Nature Mental Health Counseling, PLLC. All Rights Reserved

SESSION 11

COMMUNITY

WHY IS THIS IMPORTANT?
When clients engage in Nature-Based Therapy, they often begin to feel their place in this larger web of life—not in a hierarchical or self-centered way, but in a relational way. Sitting quietly beside a stream, tending to a garden, walking mindfully through a forest—all of these interventions offer more than calm; they offer orientation to a living world. They whisper, *you belong. You are part of this.*

WHAT YOU NEED TO KNOW IN SUPPORT OF THIS SESSION

WHAT ARE THE BENEFITS OF COMMUNITY?

- Fosters resilience through stronger relationships.
- Improves regulation and provides a sense of belonging.
- Aids mirroring and meaning-making for improved self-reflection and stability.

HOW DOES CORE CALM INCORPORATE COMMUNITY INTO NATURE-BASED THERAPY PRACTICE?

This Core Calm session shows your client that just as ecosystems thrive through mutual support and cooperation, humans are strengthened when they feel seen, supported, and held by others—both human and non-human. A tree draws nourishment not only from its roots, but also from the mycelial networks underground, the rain above, and the pollinators that visit its flowers. We are no different. Through community, clients can better understand themselves as they see parts of themselves in nature. Core Calm pushes the observation of the patience a stone shows, or the flexibility of the grass. These parallels are comforting.

WHAT IS COMMUNITY?

In the context of Nature-Based Therapy, community refers not only to human relationships but to a broader web of connection that includes the natural world—plants, animals, land, water, sky, and the unseen forces of life. This community is dynamic, relational, and alive. It offers a framework for understanding ourselves not as isolated individuals, but as participants in a deeply interconnected system—what many Indigenous traditions and ecological thinkers refer to as **the more-than-human world.**

©2026 Integrating Nature Mental Health Counseling, PLLC. All Rights Reserved

TREATMENT GOAL

After completing this session, the client will recognize they are connected to a natural community and embody that connection to heal the wounds of isolation, reclaim a sense of belonging, and reorient to a world that is vibrant, relational, and profoundly alive.

GOAL OF THE SESSION

Our goal for this session is to learn to belong in a world where the lifeforce is larger than the Self.

- The client will learn how Nature-Based Therapy reminds us of our connection to the natural world (not separation) as an expression of it.
- Client will define "belonging" as not something we must earn; it is something we already possess simply by being alive. The lifeforce that animates all living things—what some may call spirit, energy, or the pulse of the Earth—is the same force that breathes through us.
- The client will understand that:
    - Belonging is ecological. It arises from recognizing our place in a larger system of interdependence.
    - Belonging is spiritual. It is a felt sense of meaning and purpose in relation to something greater.
    - Belonging is somatic. It lives in the body when we feel rooted, supported, and safe within our environment.

©2026 Integrating Nature Mental Health Counseling, PLLC. All Rights Reserved

SESSION 11 - ACTIVITIES

CATEGORY	Introductory	Integrative and Embodied

Activity 11:1 Roots of Connection - Relationship with the Living World

Purpose: To foster nervous system regulation and introduce a felt sense of connection to the natural world by grounding in breath, body, and place.

Time: 15 minutes

Focus: ***Learning***

This practice supports your client in establishing a sense of calm, presence, and relational connection by engaging breath and sensory awareness in a natural setting. As an advanced practice into building community, the activity gently guides the client to experience themselves as part of a living system—connected to land, elements, and non-human life.

Therapist Preparation:

- **Site Selection:** Choose a quiet, undisturbed location in nature that offers visible signs of life (trees, insects, plant movement, birdsong). Avoid high-traffic areas or spaces where environmental distractions might overpower the experience.
- **Framing the Practice:** Before beginning, explain to your client that this activity is about settling the body and building awareness of their place in the living world. Use language that connects nervous system regulation with connection and belonging.
- **Posture Options:** Encourage a seated posture on the ground, a log, or a flat stone. The client may also lie down if appropriate.
- **Minimal Verbal Cueing:** Use pauses and natural pacing instead of continuous prompting. Allow the setting itself to guide the experience.

Client Engagement Steps:

1. **Orient the Client:** Briefly explain that the intention here is to settle through breath and body awareness while opening to a larger sense of connection. Let your client know this is an internal practice - there's no goal other than to *notice*.

2. **Support Arrival Through Breath:** Invite your client to slow their breath and turn inward. Model the shift by regulating your own breath and posture. Sit alongside the client for a few moments. Both of you breathing in stillness.
   Offer the prompt: *"Let your body arrive fully here, supported by the earth beneath you. Feel the weight of your limbs settle, as if there is no boundary between you and the space. Let your breath move in and out effortlessly."*

3. **Encourage Sensory Focus:** Encourage your client to select a nearby natural object—a plant, tree, or patch of earth—and spend time simply observing it, without judgment. After at least 1-2 minutes of quiet.
   - You could offer the prompt: *"Notice how this living thing simply exists—just being. Can you allow yourself to become a part of this space just as the plant/tree exists here in community, can you allow yourself todo the same?*

4. **Widen Environmental Awareness:** After still observation, encourage your client to silently broaden their awareness the surrounding space, notice temperature, movement of air, ambient sounds, or the position of the sun. Use the prompt. *"Let yourself notice the full presence of this place. You're not just here—you are part of it."*

5. **Shift to Body Awareness:** Without directing a detailed body scan, invite the client to notice internal sensations—any place that feels tight, heavy, light, or calm. Trust their body's internal rhythm and avoid over-instruction.

6. **Allow Quiet Integration:** Remain in silence together for several minutes. Allow the client to rest into stillness and feel their place in the space, not as an observer, but as a participant in the living system around them.

©2026 Integrating Nature Mental Health Counseling, PLLC. All Rights Reserved

SESSION 11 - **ACTIVITIES**

CATEGORY	Introductory	Integrative and Embodied

Activity 11:1 Roots of Connection - Relationship with the Living World (Continued)

7. **Reorient to Shared Space:** When appropriate, gently invite the client to return their gaze outward and reconnect with the present space. Begin with simple physical movement—stretching fingers, adjusting posture—and let the body lead the transition. If reflection feels appropriate, you could ask questions such as:
   - "Would you like to share anything that you noticed?"
   - "What was it like to sit in relationship with this place?"

Clinical Framing & Ongoing Practice

- Introduces grounding as both a regulatory and relational practice.
- Builds somatic awareness while strengthening the felt sense of connection to the natural world.
- Cultivates belonging by reframing the self as part of a living, interconnected whole.
- Supports clients experiencing loneliness, disconnection, or disembodiment.
- Offers a foundation for later work on ecological grief, relational repair, or purpose-finding.
- Can be used to open sessions or anchor transitions into deeper work.

Activity 11:2 Living Threads – Weaving a Tapestry of Belonging

Purpose: Applying the concept of community and belonging through collaborative, embodied practice.

Time: 45 minutes

Focus: ***Applying & Becoming***

This practice invites your client to explore the theme of community by gathering natural materials and weaving them into a symbolic tapestry. Through creative design the client externalizes their understanding of connection, belonging, and interdependence. The shared process encourages reflection on the people, qualities, and systems that support them

Therapist Preparation:

- **Collect Materials:** Colored, all-natural/organic raffia ribbon (4-5 colors).
- **Choose a Natural Setting:** Select a private location with space for easy movement, collection, and shared creation.
- **Frame as Shared Process:** Let the client know that you'll be co-creating the art together and that the emphasis is on the process, not the final product. Maintain presence through attunement rather than interpretation.

Client Engagement Steps:

1. **Set Intentions:** Begin by introducing the practice as a way to apply previous insights about connection, community, and identity through movement and making.

2. **Guide a Local Exploration:** Invite your client to walk through the landscape and identify some curious natural items, life forms, and or structures/shapes that stand out to them. Suggest they focus on texture, flexibility, or personal resonance. These materials may hold symbolic meaning or simply serve as a structure.

3. **Begin Creating Art:** Hand your client the colored strands of raffia. Explain that the activity will allow them the opportunity to create a living piece of art that represents their own living community.

- They will choose the items/life forms and natural structures (roots of trees, funny-shaped branches, flowers, rocks, etc.) to symbolize a *person, concept, or system* in your personal community that you feel supported by.

©2026 Integrating Nature Mental Health Counseling, PLLC. All Rights Reserved

SESSION 11 - **ACTIVITIES**

CATEGORY	Introductory	Integrative and Embodied

Activity 11:2 Living Threads – Weaving a Tapestry of Belonging (Continued)

- They will tie or "tag" a colored piece of raffia ribbon to the life form or natural structures they've chosen. As they "tag", they may name aloud or make notes about the person, concept, or system they are representing. For example: *"I am tying this red ribbon to this small sapling to represent my child because..."*
- They may "tag" as many natural objects or life forms as they like, but should have a minimum of seven.

4. **Support Optional Symbolic Placement:** Support your client in naming or attributing meaning to certain pieces or sections. Avoid prompting interpretation; instead, reflect back any insights the client shares naturally.

- Once their art begins to take shape, pause occasionally to observe together. Invite the client to notice any patterns, shapes, or shifts in their design process.
- Use observation as a means of inviting curiosity rather than explanation.
- **Tip:** Maybe correlate a color with category representation (i.e., red represents family or yellow represents a system)

5. **Include a Final Connection Strand:** Offer the idea of adding one final strand to represent their connection to the more-than-human world. This may be a gesture toward nature, spirit, land, or ancestry—whatever feels aligned with the client's worldview.

6. **Journaling or Verbal Reflection:** After the weaving is complete, invite the client to reflect through journaling or a brief discussion.

- Suggested prompts include:
  - What connections did this process help clarify?
  - Where do you feel most supported in your life?
  - What aspects of community are you actively building or longing for?

Clinical Framing & Ongoing Practice

- Embodies the concept of community through collaborative construction.
- Reinforces somatic and symbolic awareness of interconnectedness.
- Supports reflection on both human and ecological systems of belonging.
- Offers a flexible and creative format for externalizing support systems.
- Can be reintroduced in later sessions as a measure of growth or relational change.

My notes or thoughts for implementing this session:

©2026 Integrating Nature Mental Health Counseling, PLLC. All Rights Reserved

NOTES & TAKEAWAYS

My Thoughts & Reflections:

©2026 Integrating Nature Mental Health Counseling, PLLC. All Rights Reserved

SESSION 12

RITE OF PASSAGE

WHY IS THIS IMPORTANT?

A rite of passage holds importance in therapy as it symbolically marks a transition from distress to healing, fostering a sense of achievement and confidence in clients. As a form of ceremony, it provides closure to past experiences and integrates new identities and experiences. By tapping into cultural or personal significance, a rite of passage enriches the therapeutic journey, making it more meaningful and relevant for the client.

WHAT YOU NEED TO KNOW IN SUPPORT OF THIS SESSION

WHAT ARE THE BENEFITS OF A RITE OF PASSAGE?

- Facilitates psychological growth and maturity by marking essential life transitions.
- Strengthens cultural connections and fosters a sense of identity and belonging.
- Promotes personal development, resilience, and self-discovery through challenges and tests.
- Provides opportunity to be supported and strengthened through sharing in this experience.

HOW DOES CORE CALM INCORPORATE USE A RITE OF PASSAGE IN NATURE-BASED THERAPY?

Using a rite of passage symbolically marks a major and final achievement for your client and the conclusion of their healing journey through this program. This is a time for reflection, gratitude, and celebration.

WHAT IS A RIGHT OF PASSAGE?

"A ritual that marks a specific life transition, such as birth, menarche, marriage, or death, or a milestone such as a bar mitzvah, graduation, or admission to a new profession or association. In many prescientific societies, such rites are considered essential if the individual is to make a successful transition from one status to another. The persistence of rites of passage in modern secular societies where there is no such belief suggests that they can fulfill an important psychosocial function for both the individual and the social group."

American Psychological Association

©2026 Integrating Nature Mental Health Counseling, PLLC. All Rights Reserved

TREATMENT GOAL

After completing this session, the client will gain closure and reflection, promoting gratitude, leadership, and a sense of community.

GOALS OF THE SESSION

Our goal for this session is to reflect on and celebrate the client's personal healing journey throughout these 12 sessions.

- The client will be able to practice resisting the urge to suppress any arising emotions; rather, they will observe, express and acknowledge them.
- The client will recognize today as the culmination of many successes and challenges over thier time in the Core Calm program. It is a time to honor their transitions and healing.
- The client will be able to express gratitude for their journey, the growth, and the transformation that has taken place within them.

©2026 Integrating Nature Mental Health Counseling, PLLC. All Rights Reserved

SESSION 12 - ACTIVITIES

Final Activity: Crossing the Threshold – A Rite of Passage in Nature

Purpose: To mark the culmination of the client's therapeutic journey, honoring the growth, healing, and transformation that have taken place over the course of the program. This closing rite of passage invites the client to reflect on the self they are leaving behind, to symbolically cross into a new phase of being, and to celebrate their emergence as a more resilient, aware, and connected individual—one who belongs to the living world.

Time: 60 minutes

Therapist Preparation:

- **Gather Materials:**
  - Tree seedling or a native plant
  - Small trowel
  - Water for planting
  - Optional natural items for celebration (feather, flower, raffia ribbon, stone)
  - Natural drawing or writing tools (optional)
- **Create a Ceremonial Space:** Choose a quiet, private area with a visible natural threshold—this could be a bend in the trail, the edge of a clearing, a stone crossing, or a symbolic arch made from branches or a split between two trees. Ensure the space has two clearly defined areas to mark "past" and "future," with enough distance between to hold the gravity of the crossing.
- **Therapeutic Framing:** Hold this session with reverence. Let your presence signal that this is not a typical exercise, but a ceremony. Honor silence *or* celebrate creativity, and the land itself as a co-facilitator of transformation. **Tip:** You might enjoy adorning yourself with special items or wearing a "celebratory-style" garment to mark the specialness of the occasion that is unique to your client.

PART 1: Honoring the Past (15 minutes)

1. **Prepare the Client for Ceremony:** Invite your client into the ceremonial space. Frame the session with care: *"You've spent the past twelve weeks doing deep, courageous work. Today, we honor that. This ceremony is not just an ending—it's a transition. You are not the same person who began this journey."*

2. **Create a Symbol of the Past Self:** On one side of the threshold, invite your client to reflect on the version of themselves that is being left behind. This may include pain, limiting beliefs, outdated patterns, or past roles.

- Encourage them to gather nearby natural materials—stones for heaviness, leaves for old narratives, tangled grass for confusion—and arrange them into a symbol or sculpture that represents the past.
- As they move about the gathering process, engage them in discussion of their process and their selection, if it feels appropriate to do so.

©2026 Integrating Nature Mental Health Counseling, PLLC. All Rights Reserved

SESSION 12 - **ACTIVITIES**

3. **Optional Integration Through Writing or Art:** If your client wishes, offer charcoal, natural pigment, or a small piece of paper for drawing or writing. They may write a word, a name, or draw an image on a piece of paper or a flat rock, which represents what they are leaving behind.

4. **Pause and Witness:** Allow your client to sit quietly with the symbol of their past self. Offer silent witnessing.
- After 60-90 seconds, acknowledge the emotional weight and significance of this part of the process.
- Encourage your client to explain what they have created and why.

PART 2: Crossing the Threshold (15 minutes)

5. **Approach the Threshold:** Invite your client to stand at the edge of the threshold. You may choose to mark it physically—a line of stones, a fallen branch, a woven vine arch, colorful raffia or fabrics (which should be removed after the ceremony).

6. **Cross with Intention:** When your client is ready, invite them to step slowly and intentionally across the threshold. This crossing can be silent, spoken, or even ritualized with a gesture (e.g., laying down a leaf, stepping barefoot, or pausing to breathe deeply).

7. **Welcome to the Arrival:** On the other side, honor the crossing by offering a gesture of celebration:
- Hand your client a feather, flower, or ribbon.
- Offer a warm gaze or bow.
- Place a hand gently on your own heart.
- Beating of a drum or clapping. Even a cheer!

PART 3: Embodying the Future (25 minutes)

8. **Create a Symbol of Becoming**: Now, on the "future" side, invite your client to create a new symbol representing the self they are becoming. This may include strengths, clarity, relationships, purpose, or values they now embody.
- Encourage the use of soft grasses for flexibility, upright branches for strength, or flowers for openness. This symbol is a declaration of what is alive in them now.

9. **Planting the Seedling**: Guide your client in selecting a place to plant their tree seedling. Frame this as a living mirror of their transformation—a being that will grow, root, and exist long after this session ends.
- As they plant, offer a ceremonial reflection: *"This tree is you, rooted in the earth, part of the living world, still growing. You are not alone in your becoming. You are part of a greater web of life."*
- Support them in watering the soil, pressing the earth down, and offering a final word, breath, or intention to the plant.

10. **Silent Integration:** Invite your client to sit with the planted seedling and their symbol of becoming. Offer 60-90 seconds of quiet reflection, gratitude, and coalescence.

My notes or thoughts for implementing this session:

©2026 Integrating Nature Mental Health Counseling, PLLC. All Rights Reserved

SESSION 12 - **ACTIVITIES**

Closing the Ceremony

1. **Ritual Completion:** To mark the end of the ceremony for your client, you will offer one final symbolic act:

- A simple spoken affirmation
- A stone placed at the roots of the tree
- A circle drawn around the planting site
- A quiet walk together to return from the threshold

2. **Optional Final Reflection Prompts:** If your client is open to sharing or journaling, you may offer a prompt such as:
    - *"What are you taking with you? What are you most proud of within yourself?"*
    - *"What does your growth mean in this larger world?"*
    - *"What are you becoming?"*

- Offer your sincere acknowledgment:
  "Thank you for the work you've done. Thank you for becoming."

Clinical Framing & Ongoing Practice

- Marks the culmination of a full therapeutic journey with reverence and embodiment.
- Offers integration of emotional, cognitive, relational, and ecological growth.
- Provides a physical, living representation of personal transformation.
- Reinforces the client's identity as a resilient, interconnected being.
- Serves as a ceremonial anchor that the client can return to mentally and symbolically over time.
- Encourages ongoing reflection, tending, and connection with both self and nature.

©2026 Integrating Nature Mental Health Counseling, PLLC. All Rights Reserved

NOTES & TAKEAWAYS

My Thoughts & Reflections:

©2026 Integrating Nature Mental Health Counseling, PLLC. All Rights Reserved

GLOSSARY

Active Engagement
A therapeutic approach emphasizing direct participation in structured, experiential activities. In Nature-Based Therapy, active engagement supports skill acquisition, increases motivation, and facilitates embodied learning through interaction with the natural environment.

Awareness
The capacity to consciously observe internal experiences (thoughts, emotions, bodily sensations) and external surroundings. Awareness is foundational to self-regulation and is cultivated through intentional attention and sensory engagement.

Behavioral Activation
A therapeutic strategy that encourages individuals to engage in meaningful activities to counter patterns of avoidance, withdrawal, or depression. In nature-based contexts, this often involves purposeful movement and interaction with the environment.

Cognitive Behavioral Therapy (CBT)
An evidence-based therapeutic approach focused on identifying, challenging, and modifying maladaptive thought patterns and behaviors. Within this curriculum, CBT principles are integrated with experiential and nature-based practices.

Cognitive Flexibility
The ability to shift perspective, adapt thinking, and generate alternative interpretations of experiences. This skill supports resilience, problem-solving, and emotional regulation.

Cognitive Load
The total amount of mental effort being used at a given time. High cognitive load can impair attention, decision-making, and emotional regulation, particularly in individuals experiencing stress or trauma.

Cognitive Reframing
A CBT-based technique that involves identifying and restructuring unhelpful or distorted thinking patterns to develop more balanced and adaptive perspectives.

Core Calm™
A structured Nature-Based Therapy (NBT) curriculum designed to support trauma recovery, emotional regulation, and personal growth through experiential engagement with the natural world.

Distress Tolerance
The ability to endure and manage emotional discomfort without becoming overwhelmed or engaging in maladaptive coping behaviors. Often developed through gradual exposure and skill-building practices.

Ecotherapy
A therapeutic approach that involves intentional interaction with natural environments to promote psychological, emotional, and physical well-being. It emphasizes the healing potential of human–nature relationships.

Embodiment
The experience of being present in and connected to one's body. Embodied practices increase awareness of physical sensations and support integration of emotional and cognitive processes.

Emotional Regulation
The ability to identify, understand, and modulate emotional responses in a way that supports adaptive functioning and well-being.

Experiential Learning
A process of learning through direct experience, reflection, and application. In this curriculum, learning occurs through engagement with nature-based activities rather than passive instruction.

Grounding
Techniques that anchor attention in the present moment, often through sensory awareness (e.g., sight, touch, sound). Grounding supports emotional regulation and reduces anxiety or dissociation.

Human–Nature Connection
The reciprocal relationship between individuals and the natural world. This connection supports identity development, emotional regulation, and overall well-being.

Identity
An individual's sense of self, shaped by experiences, beliefs, values, and relationships. Identity development is explored through reflection and experiential processes.

Integration
The process of incorporating new insights, skills, and experiences into daily life and one's sense of self. Integration supports lasting behavioral and psychological change.

©2026 Integrating Nature Mental Health Counseling, PLLC. All Rights Reserved

Interoception
The awareness of internal bodily states, such as heartbeat, breath, and physical tension. Interoceptive awareness supports emotional insight and regulation.

Mindfulness
The practice of intentionally focusing attention on the present moment with openness, curiosity, and without judgment. Mindfulness is a core skill across all sessions.

Nature-Based Therapy (NBT)
A clinical approach that integrates evidence-based therapeutic practices with direct engagement in natural environments. NBT emphasizes experiential learning, sensory awareness, and the therapeutic role of the natural world in healing and growth.

Nervous System Regulation
The process of stabilizing physiological and emotional responses by balancing activation (sympathetic nervous system) and relaxation (parasympathetic nervous system).

Psychoeducation
The process of providing individuals with information about psychological concepts, mental health, and coping strategies to increase understanding and support skill development.

Problem-Solving
The ability to identify challenges, generate options, and implement effective solutions. Nature-based activities often provide real-time opportunities to practice this skill.

Reflection
The intentional process of reviewing experiences to extract meaning, increase insight, and support learning and growth.

Release (Emotional Release)
The process of letting go of emotional, cognitive, or physical tension. In NBT, release may occur through symbolic, physical, or expressive practices.

Resilience
The capacity to adapt, recover, and grow in response to adversity, stress, or challenge. Resilience is developed through exposure, skill-building, and supportive experiences.

Rite of Passage
A structured or symbolic experience that marks a transition from one stage of life, identity, or understanding to another. Often used to support closure and integration.

Self-Awareness
The ability to recognize and understand one's own thoughts, emotions, behaviors, and internal processes

Self-Efficacy
An individual's belief in their ability to successfully manage challenges and achieve desired outcomes.

Self-Reflection
The deliberate examination of one's thoughts, behaviors, and experiences to gain insight and promote personal growth.

Sensory Awareness
The practice of tuning into sensory input (sight, sound, touch, smell) to increase presence and grounding.

Social Connection
The experience of feeling supported, understood, and connected to others. In NBT, this includes connection with both people and the natural environment.

Stress
The body's physiological and psychological response to perceived demands or threats. While adaptive in short bursts, chronic stress can negatively impact health and functioning.

Symbolic Practice
Therapeutic activities that use metaphor or representation (e.g., building, releasing, creating) to process internal experiences and facilitate insight.

Trauma
A psychological and physiological response to overwhelming or distressing experiences that exceed an individual's capacity to cope.

Trauma Recovery
The process of healing from the effects of trauma through safe, supportive, and integrative therapeutic interventions.

Values
Core beliefs and principles that guide behavior, decision-making, and a sense of purpose.

©2026 Integrating Nature Mental Health Counseling, PLLC. All Rights Reserved

INDEX

F

Focus, 80-88
Forest Bathing for Mindful Awareness, 52-53

©2026 Integrating Nature Mental Health Counseling, PLLC. All Rights Reserved

P

R

S

T

V

W

©2026 Integrating Nature Mental Health Counseling, PLLC. All Rights Reserved

www.ingramcontent.com/pod-product-compliance
Lightning Source LLC
LaVergne TN
LVHW070954210926
848482LV00002B/211